# JEWELRY MAKING

# JEWELRY MAKING
## *for the amateur*

KLARES LEWES

Illustrated by Karin Ann Lewes

LONDON: B. T. BATSFORD LIMITED
NEW YORK: REINHOLD PUBLISHING CORPORATION

FIRST PUBLISHED, 1965
LIBRARY OF CONGRESS CATALOG CARD NO. 65–28050

MADE AND PRINTED IN GREAT BRITAIN BY
JARROLD AND SONS LTD, LONDON AND NORWICH,
FOR THE PUBLISHERS B. T. BATSFORD LTD,
4 FITZHARDINGE ST, PORTMAN SQ., LONDON W.I
REINHOLD PUBLISHING CORPORATION, 430 PARK AVENUE,
NEW YORK 10022

# Contents

# *Acknowledgment*

The Author and Publishers wish to thank the following for permission to reproduce the illustrations appearing in this book:

The Worshipful Company of Goldsmiths, for figs. 28, 47, 48, 66, 76, 106, 130 and 131.

The Ewan Phillips Gallery, Maddox Street, London W.1, for figs. 17, 29, 79 and 94, and the three brooches reproduced on the back of the jacket.

Miss Michelle Connolly, for fig. 36.

# The Illustrations

# INTRODUCTION

## *Jewelry Making for the Amateur*

Jewelry? Made by an amateur? Until very recent years the idea would have been unthinkable, for the accepted notion of jewelry was of something so delicate and ornate that no amateur, with only his spare time available for practice, could ever hope to achieve the high standard of workmanship required.

Modern taste, here as elsewhere, has changed. Where formerly the stress was on elaborately intricate detail whose main purpose often was merely to display a stone of standardised cut, today the best jewelry tends to be simple and plain; its elegance is based on subtlety of line and form, and on surface treatment or texture. The lead here has been given most strikingly by the many modern artists, painters and especially sculptors, who have been fascinated by the possibilities offered by jewelry. They include Picasso, Arp, Lipschitz, Lurçat, Giacometti, Lynn Chadwick, Mary Kessell, José Rivera, Victor Pasmore and Georges Braque to name but a few.

The new taste makes the craft technically more accessible to the amateur, since construction is simplified. But by the same token it calls for a much higher standard of design if the result is to be satisfying. This is no doubt, in part at any rate, the reason for the great vitality of modern work. It is also one of the factors which gives the craft its appeal for the amateur, since he can face the challenge to his imagination and inventiveness in the knowledge that he need not be frustrated because he does not possess an unattainable standard of technical skill.

There is another factor. The shop-bought article is made by an unknown craftsman for an unknown wearer. The average piece in fact will have been mass-produced for a mass market.

The amateur, however, has the extraordinary satisfaction of being able to design with a special person in view, whose particular character and characteristics he can serve with his particular piece of jewelry. This is how one produces—or tries to produce—'compulsive' jewelry, the piece that makes people say to its wearer: this is you!

The space required is small—enough for a work-bench or table. The essential tools are few: one or two hammers, some files, a piercing-saw, a soldering flame using ordinary gas or bottled gas, a drill, two or three pliers, a steel block and a lead block and one or two more. With these one can go a pretty long way, but of course more will be added from time to time, some very useful—others rather less, serving little more in fact than the enthusiast's natural self-indulgence—but at least he will never be saddled with mere gadgets, for none is made.

The basic processes which have to be learnt are also few, and being physically light they are well within the capabilities of a woman. One must learn to saw out shapes in thin metal sheet, bend and form them, drill holes, twist and bend wires, join pieces by soldering, use a file and a hammer. There is nothing difficult about them, but they have to be practised and learnt well. It is in reality your own two hands holding a few simple light tools, and guided by your own two eyes, patiently and painstakingly, which constitute your technical equipment. And that is the equipment, essentially unchanged today, which has given us the wonderful jewelry dating back hundreds and thousands of years, which we can admire in our great museums.

They are worth studying, those pieces. The amateur will do so with more under-standing after he has learnt something of the craft, and with a budding feeling of kinship: for it is a pleasant dream—but not wholly a dream—that he will himself one day produce a masterpiece. And if he does not, at least what he makes will be worn, and will give pleasure.

# CHAPTER I

## *The Materials*

Jewelry making is one of the metal-working crafts. The jeweller is really (though he sometimes forgets it) a goldsmith, a silversmith—or even, nowadays, a blacksmith. He may use other materials, ivory, enamels, precious stones and stones not precious at all; seldom, however, by themselves: they are used to decorate, or be set off by, some construction in metal.

It is vital, therefore, to learn how to handle metals, which means to learn what can and what cannot, or at any rate ought not to be done with any given metal. So important is this that there are craftsmen who so to speak specialise in one metal and will not handle others at all, or only under protest. There is one master craftsman who nowadays makes prototype models from which bracelet charms will be cast in thousands. His models are made in 18 carat gold, though there is no reason other than his insistence why they should not be made in 14 carat or 9 carat, in silver, brass or copper. His attitude represents a craftsman's pride and self-respect, but it also expresses his consciousness that he can work best in 18 carat gold because that is the material he understands best.

In this chapter we shall describe the characteristics of the metals useful in jewelry making. 'Getting the feel of them', of course, will come only from handling them, and from using the processes which we describe later.

All the metals can be obtained in the form of sheet, wire, rod, bar or tube, in a large range of sizes or gauges, and shapes. Sheet is always sheet, but wire can be round or square, and in the case of the precious metals, triangular, half-round, rectangular, oval, etc. Rod and bar are merely the larger sizes of wire. Tube is usually round, but can also be square or oval, and is made not only in different diameters or outside measurements, but also with different wall thicknesses.

When buying, one must specify the dimensions. For sheet and round wire, standard gauges have been established, though as is common in any system based on English weights and measures, the standards show no apparent logic in their arrangements. Moreover, there are many of them. Thus we find the Birmingham Metal Gauge (Shakespeare's) and the Dial Gauge for sheet, and for wire two Birmingham Wire Gauges, namely Stubb's and Shakespeare's, and also the Standard Wire Gauge. The Americans, likewise, have several standards, some inherited from England. Fortunately in both countries some are more standard, or rather more commonly used, than others: in England it is the Birmingham Metal Gauge (B.M.G.) for sheet and the Standard Wire Gauge (S.W.G.) for round wire; in America it is the Brown and

Sharpe Gauge (B. & S.) for both. Appendix I is a table showing the relation between these and their equivalents in inch and millimetre.

The metals are always priced by weight. For the precious metals the basis is the ounce troy, with 20 pennyweights (dwt) to the ounce, and 12 ounces to the pound (which is the same as the pound avoirdupois). However, there is now a tendency to weigh the precious metals in ounces and decimals of an ounce, which is easier to understand than pennyweights and the 24 grains which make up a pennyweight.

From the point of view of the metallurgist there are many characteristics of metals which matter. From our point of view, there are few. Colour is important, since the product is to be decorative. Resistance to tarnish and corrosion is also important, partly for the same reason and partly because this affects durability. Lastly, for the craftsman there is workability, a word which covers malleability, ductility and toughness.

Malleability is the metal's responsiveness when hammered or rolled to stretching without cracking or breaking. It is this property which enables the metal to be shaped by beating it or passing it between rollers. Gold is the most malleable of all metals: it can be hammered into gold leaf that is less than a millionth of an inch thick and semi-transparent.

Ductility is responsiveness to being drawn into fine wire and here again gold is pre-eminent: one gram of it, it is said, can be drawn into a wire three miles long and much, much finer than a hair. Lead, on the other hand, though it is very malleable, has no ductility; it cannot be drawn into wire.

Toughness is the ability to support bending and twisting without breaking; it is thus not the same thing as malleability or ductility, though toughness is involved in both these characteristics in that it represents their extreme limits.

Workability varies with each of the metals. Its various aspects can, and for various purposes such as engineering must, be defined in scientific terms, but to the jeweller such definitions are useless. It is only by handling the metals that he learns not only how to shape them, but how much shaping they will take, and how in this respect they differ from each other.

There is one other characteristic which should be mentioned at this stage, and that is 'work-hardening'. When shaping metals, by bending, hammering, twisting, etc., stresses are set up which result in the metal becoming harder than normal. This is known as work-hardening, and the stage is ultimately reached when further working becomes difficult or impossible: the metal responds by fracturing. At this stage the metal must be 'annealed'. It is heated to a certain temperature, then cooled either quickly or slowly according to the metal, and this process properly carried out relieves the stresses and restores the original workability.

Annealing in the case of most metals results in the formation of surface oxides which appear as a stain or even as scale. These oxides must be removed by 'pickling' the article in a 10 per cent solution of sulphuric acid. This pickling can often be combined with the cooling off stage, the article after heating simply being dropped into the acid. Since a 10 per cent solution is relatively weak (though still strong enough to burn holes in clothes), it pays to warm it up with the metal in it, for this speeds up the action very much, reducing to a few minutes what otherwise might take several hours.

Work-hardening, however, is also a useful property. Silver, for instance, in its normal state is too soft for certain purposes. A brooch-pin would not support its brooch but would bend. The solid collar shown in the illustration (15) would become distorted when being put on and taken off. If, however, the piece can be worked after being completed, by twisting in the case of the brooch-pin or gentle hammering in the case of the collar, it will become sufficiently hard for its purpose.

## COPPER

Copper is a soft, malleable and ductile material, very easy to shape and handle, and also relatively cheap. It is thus particularly suitable for the beginner, for a successful effort can be retained, and worn, with pleasure; and a failure can be scrapped without a pang. Being as soft as it is, however, and easily bent and distorted, it must be used in relatively heavy sections and is not well suited to very delicate construction for which silver and gold would be perfectly serviceable: but this is in any case not work which the beginner would tackle.

Its rich red colour gives it decorative value of a high order. Unfortunately it tarnishes easily, but its surface can be protected by applying a colourless cellulose lacquer such as clear nail varnish (though this does detract somewhat from its appearance). Alternatively the surface can be deliberately oxidised by treatment with chemicals so as to produce black, brown, and green tones (see p. 48), or it can be plated in silver or gold. Copper is excellent as a base for enamelled work.

Anneal by heating uniformly to a dull red colour and quench in water or pickle.

## GILDING METAL

Gilding metal is really a form of brass, an alloy of 80–95 per cent copper and 20–5 per cent zinc. Its colour is more nearly gold and in one of its forms, pinchbeck (88 per cent copper, 12 per cent zinc) it is well known as an imitation gold in Victorian jewelry. Its advantages over copper are that it is tougher, though still very malleable, and that it does not oxidise and tarnish so quickly.

Anneal like copper.

## GERMAN SILVER

German silver, or nickel silver as it is also known, owes its name not to the presence of silver, of which it has none, but to its colour which approximates that of silver, though with a slightly yellowish tone. It is an alloy of copper, usually 60 per cent, and zinc and nickel, 20 per cent each.

It is much tougher and more springy than gilding metal, silver or gold, and is thus harder to work. This (plus the fact that it is cheaper than gilding metal because of its lower copper content) is no doubt the reason why silversmith apprentices are often started with this metal.

Because of its toughness, German silver wire is often used for brooch-pins.

Anneal like copper.

## SILVER

Silver is perhaps the most useful of all metals for the amateur jeweller; mainly, of course, because although it is one of the precious metals, its cost is only a fraction that of gold. For malleability and ductility it is second only to gold, and it is superbly responsive to polishing and other surface treatment.

*Fine silver*, which is the pure form, is actually too soft for articles intended for everyday use, but it is often employed to make the bezels for stone settings: these are usually protected from wear by their position, and since bezels have to be turned down over the edge of the stone to hold it, the extra softness of the fine silver is desirable.

For all other work, *standard* or *sterling* silver is used. This is an alloy of silver and a base metal, usually copper in the proportion—fixed by law—of 925 parts of silver to 75 parts of the alloy. The alloy gives the hardness that is needed for wear. Sterling has been the accepted standard since 1560. It was superseded in 1696 by an even higher standard (introduced in order to discourage the melting down of silver coin) made up of 958 parts of silver to 42 parts of alloy. This was known as *Britannia* silver and had its own hallmark. The standard was abolished in 1719, but it is still obtainable and still receives the appropriate mark. Its use nowadays is mainly for reproduction silver ware of the period.

Annealing heat is a very dull red—best judged if the heating is done in a subdued light. The article should then be allowed to cool slightly before being quenched in pickle.

It is wise not to overheat, nor to heat too often, for this results in oxidation which shows itself in the form of a dark stain known as fire-stain, which can be difficult to remove. The normal method is to heat evenly to dull red, then pickle in hot acid. Repeat three times. This dissolves all the surface oxide and leaves a very thin skin of pure silver. Since any further work such as filing or smoothing with emery paper would break through this skin, the process is not carried out until the article is finished (save for setting of stones) and has been polished. It can then be heated and pickled as described, and a very light polish to follow will restore its shine. If this procedure is impractical, then the only alternative is to have it silver-plated.

## GOLD

Gold is gold, the most malleable and ductile of metals, and the most valued for jewelry. Like silver, it is too soft for ordinary use, and sufficiently expensive to justify a number of standards of purity. The standard is indicated by 'carat', 24 carat being *fine gold*. In England the legally recognised standards are 22 carat, 18, 14 and 9 carat, these figures representing the number of parts of gold to alloy in 24. Thus 18 carat is

18 parts out of 24, or 75 per cent gold and 25 per cent alloy. Other countries recognise slightly different standards, for instance 10 carat instead of 9 in the U.S.A. and 15 carat instead of 14 on the Continent.

The alloys used may be silver, copper, nickel and other metals, in varying proportions to produce different colours and working characteristics. The colours may be white or shades of yellow, green or red. The working characteristics may be suitability for ordinary goldsmith's work, or special suitability for making such things as brooch-pins, or for processes such as casting, spinning, enamelling, etc. The result in the case of one firm of smelters is a list of eleven varieties of 9 carat gold, six of 14 carat, eight of 18 carat and two of 22 carat—twenty-seven varieties altogether which include ten yellow (yellow, pale yellow, rich yellow and sovereign), eight white, six red (red, pale red and deep red), and lastly three green. The craftsman is well catered for.

As might be expected, since the alloys vary the annealing process will vary too and as to this it is best to seek advice from the smelter who supplies the metal. Broadly speaking, however, it is safe to heat to a dull red; thereafter most golds should be allowed to cool to black heat, which does not take long, and then quenched in water. Some varieties can be quenched immediately and there are a few which should be left to cool in the air.

# CHAPTER II
## *The Workshop*

The workshop is any space in any room that will accommodate a work-bench or table, and a shelf or two for other equipment. Good light is important, and if it is to be electric is best in the form of an adjustable lamp clamped to the bench or screwed to the wall which can be directed where it is needed.

The work-bench can be a reasonably solid kitchen table. The professional work-bench is shown in Fig. 1. Its unusual feature is the half-circle cut out of the top. The craftsman works inside this, and a leather skin is stretched underneath across the opening which serves to catch all the filings—known in the trade as *lemel*—and scraps; these, being silver or gold, are valuable and can either be melted down for re-use or sold back to the dealer in precious metals. The half-circle that has been cut out is not wasted: with the addition of three legs it forms, traditionally, the craftsman's stool.

Screwed or bolted—not merely clamped—to the bench there will be a fairly substantial engineer's vice. Two-inch parallel jaws will do, and these jaws, which are

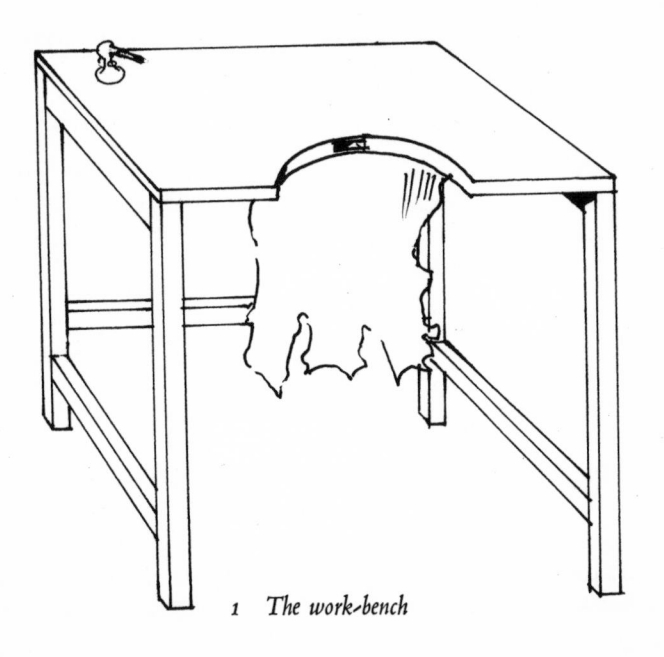

1   *The work-bench*

heavily serrated and would damage any soft metal gripped between them, should be covered by *clams*, either fibre pads slipped over, or strips of copper bent round.

Also attached to the jeweller's bench you will find a *bench-pin*, a small wooden wedge measuring about 5 × 3 inches with a sloping top and a V-shaped opening in front. It is on this that all sawing and filing is done, and the purpose of the opening is to give all-round support to the often very flimsy piece of metal that is being sawn. Bench-pins can be bought for a few pence or made up out of a piece of scrap wood, and can be screwed or clamped to the table top.

With regard to the tools, as in the case of other hobbies there is, of course, no end to them. The difference is that the jeweller's craft is entirely free of useless

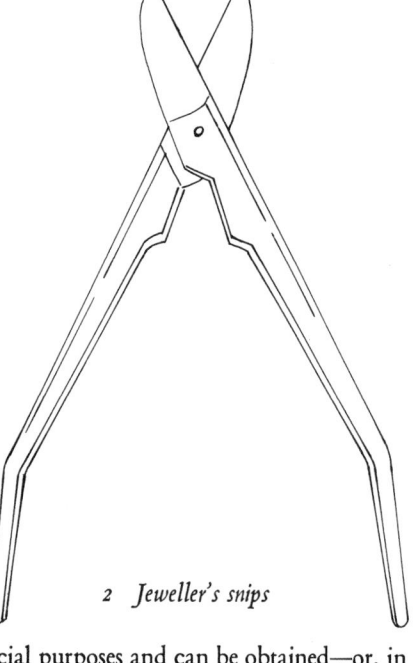

2  *Jeweller's snips*

gadgetry. Many of the tools in fact serve special purposes and can be obtained—or, in some cases, made—as and when actually needed.

The basic tools and equipment fall under the following heads: measuring, cutting, shaping, soldering, polishing and ancillary (mostly expendable).

## Measuring

A 6 inch or 12 inch engineers' steel rule; a 4 inch engineers' square (to ensure straight edges and right angles); a scriber (for drawing lines on metal); and a pair of spring dividers, 3 or 4 inch (for marking out circles and arcs on metal, or for transferring measurements).

## Cutting

Jeweller's shears (2) or tin-snips (for rough cutting sheet metal); a 4 inch adjustable piercing-saw frame, with a selection of saw blades Nos. 00, 2 and 4; a drill-stock with a set of spade drills, or alternatively a $\frac{1}{4}$ inch hand-drill with a set of twist-drills; jeweller's top or side-cutting pliers for cutting wire (3).

## Shaping

Jeweller's hammer or alternatively a light tack hammer; a No. 1 rawhide hammer or a light wooden mallet (which enables metal to be hammered without leaving

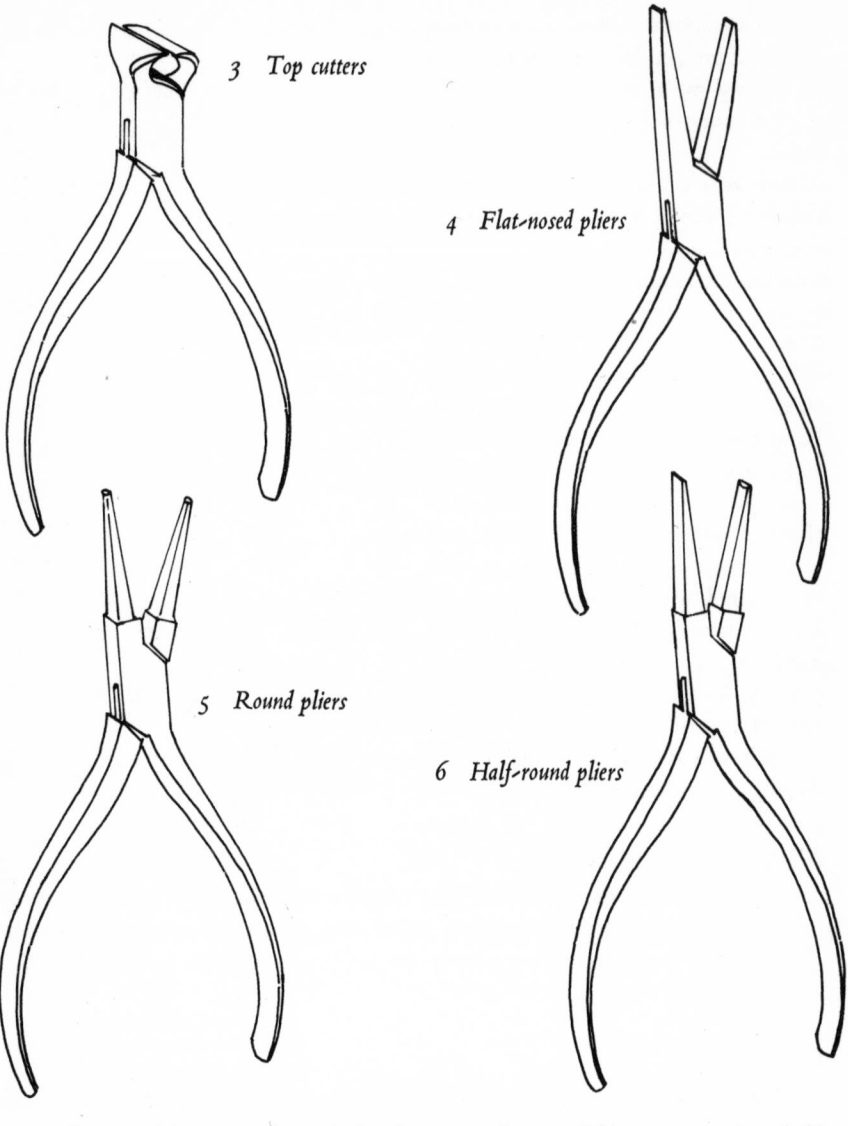

3 *Top cutters*

4 *Flat-nosed pliers*

5 *Round pliers*

6 *Half-round pliers*

surface marks); two pairs 4 inch pliers, one flat-nosed (4), one round or half-round (5, 6), the former for gripping flat metal, the latter for shaping metal to a curve; a selection of files (7), 6 or 8 inch, flat and half-round, medium, fine and smooth; a selection of needle files, fine cut, flat, crossing, triangle, round and barrette; a lead block, roughly 6 × 4 inches and about 2 inches thick (made by melting scrap lead in an iron saucepan and casting it in a suitable tin or wooden box); a steel block, about 4 inches square and 1 or $1\frac{1}{2}$ inches thick, with its face quite flat and polished on emery cloth to a mirror finish (for flattening sheet metal, plain ring shanks, etc.); a steel ring triblet (a tapered steel rod, preferably marked with ring sizes) for shaping and sizing ring shanks (8); a selection of steel rods (knitting needles, the shanks of twist drills, etc., will do) for making chain links.

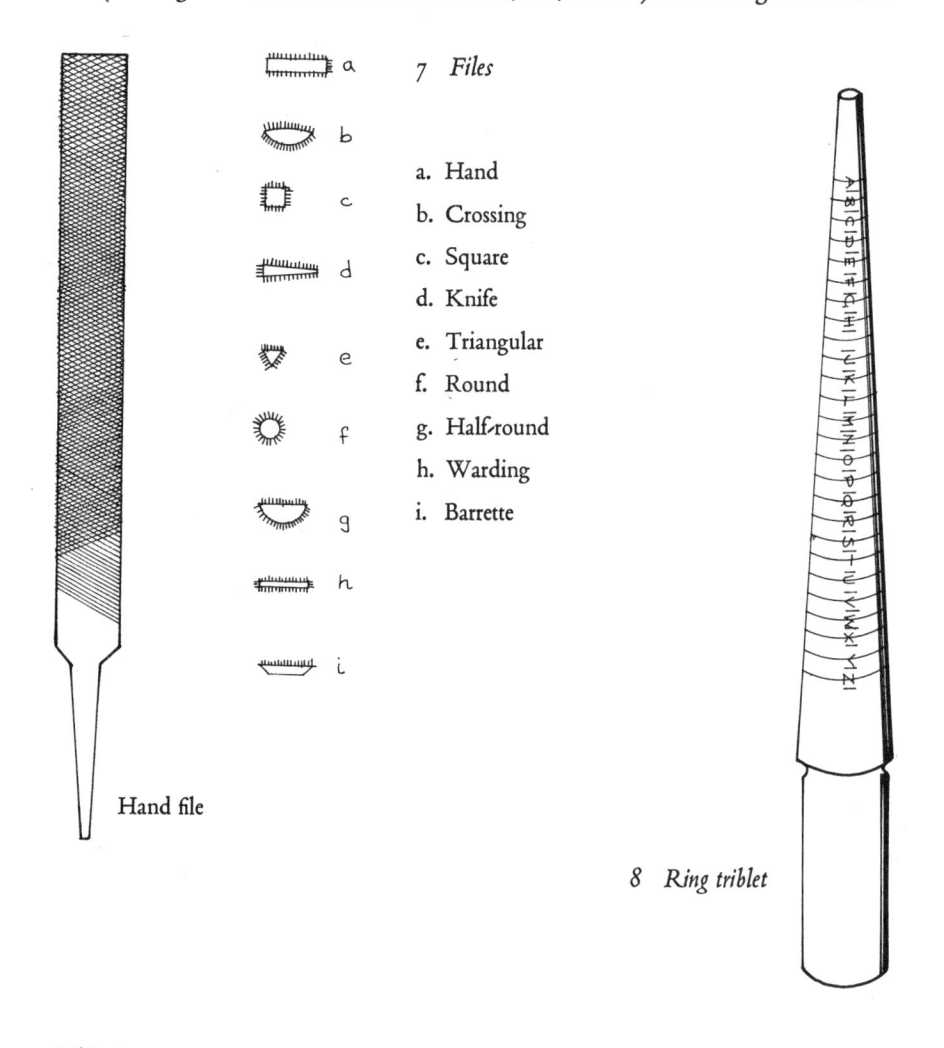

7 *Files*

a. Hand
b. Crossing
c. Square
d. Knife
e. Triangular
f. Round
g. Half-round
h. Warding
i. Barrette

Hand file

8 *Ring triblet*

## Soldering

Here the equipment depends on the source of heat you intend to use, whether it is to be ordinary gas or one of the bottled gases, such as butane or propane.

The former is probably slightly cheaper, at any rate in cost of equipment, but should be adopted only if a supply pipe is reasonably near to the work-bench. If

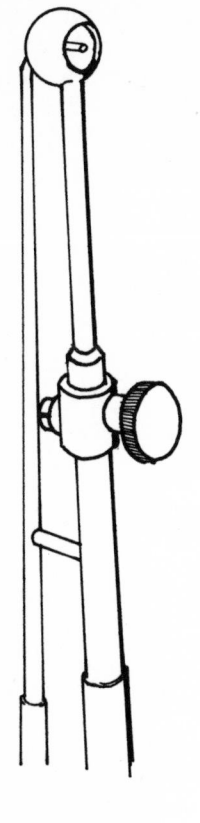

9 *Mouth
blowpipe*

this is the case, fit a tap to the bench and connect to the supply by means of a rubber pipe. You will then need a 'French' type mouth blow‐pipe (*9*). This is connected by means of a rubber tube to the tap, and is fitted with another length of tube and a mouthpiece through which air can be blown into the flame in such a way as to direct it and intensify the heat. It also has a tap to regulate the amount of gas and so control the size of flame.

The alternative is a butane or propane gas bottle which can be bought from dealers or, often, hired from the local gas company. Gas bottles are available in various sizes ($4\frac{1}{2}$ lb., which refers to the weight of the liquid gas content, being a convenient one) and are re‐fillable. In addition you will need a handpiece and nozzle and a length of connecting hose. The nozzles or burners, too, are available in various sizes, some large enough to weld ships' plates: you will need the smallest size, and perhaps one larger.

Soldering is carried out on a fireproof surface, provided by prepared charcoal or asbestos blocks available from jewellers' supply houses.

Lastly you will need a range of hard solders, and a supply of flux (p. 36).

## Polishing

The finest polishes and finishes are undoubtedly obtained by hand methods. It was 'the butler's thumb' which gave family plate its marvellous patina. But such methods are slow, and it helps to invest in a small electric motor—$\frac{1}{10}$ to $\frac{1}{4}$ horse‐power—and these can often be obtained second‐hand. You will need a variety of 'mops' to mount on the spindle of the motor, made in various grades of hardness of felt (for flat surfaces only), layers of fine calico stitched together (for shaped surfaces), and of lambswool or 'swansdown' (for final polishing). You will also need a felt 'finger' for polishing the inside of rings, and bristle brushes for carved and textured surfaces.

For hand polishing a few old toothbrushes and some pieces of chamois leather will suffice.

Lastly, a small burnisher, of steel, polished to a mirror finish, or of agate.

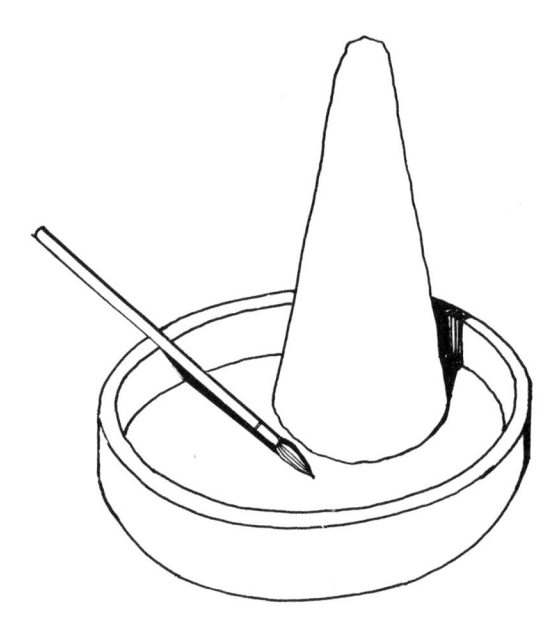

*10   Borax cone, dish and paintbrush*

## Ancillary

The ancillary equipment consists mainly of expendable materials.

For pickling, you will need a 10 per cent dilute solution of sulphuric acid. Half a litre will last a long time. The acid can be bought pure, and diluted as required. But acid is always a dangerous substance to have about, and it is better to reduce the risk by avoiding the pure acid. For the same reason it is wise to have handy a bottle of soda bicarbonate dissolved in water to neutralise any splashes or spillage. Pickling can be carried out in a small glass or china bowl, but the acid is more effective if heated and accordingly a copper pan (obtainable from a jeweller's supply house) is preferable.

For soldering a flux is needed. The traditional flux is a borax cone, rubbed down with a little water in a borax dish made of unglazed earthenware (*10*). The alternative is one of the proprietary fluxes on the market and available either in liquid or in powder form.

A box of assorted iron cotter pins, and some iron binding wire, to hold pieces in position while they are being soldered, are also useful.

For cleaning up and polishing, a supply of emery paper, say grades 4/0, 2/0 and 0, a ¼ inch and an ⅛ inch square stick of Water-of-Ayr stone (also known as 'Scotch stone'); a block of tripoli and one of rouge, together with a tin of rouge powder, metal polish and powdered whiting, complete the basic equipment.

# CHAPTER III

## *Basic Processes*

### SAWING AND PIERCING

The jeweller's saw (*11*) is a kind of miniature fretsaw. The frame may be either fixed, or adjustable in length to accommodate different lengths of saw blade. The latter feature is no doubt a survival from times when blades were not standardised in length and were fairly expensive, so that it was a saving to be able to use up broken ends. Nowadays this is hardly worth while.

More important is the depth of frame for upon this depends how far you can cut into a sheet of metal. The most useful size is 4 inches. A larger frame, say 6 inches, is not often needed; it is less rigid and lacks balance, and is therefore more difficult to control, with consequently greater risk of blade breakage and inaccurate sawing.

Blades, sold in packets of a dozen or a gross, vary in coarseness of teeth and are graded and numbered accordingly, 2, 1, 0, 2/0, 3/0, 4/0, etc., getting finer and finer. At first blush it would seem that the finer the blade, the less work is involved, simply because less metal is removed. In practice the very fine blade is harder to guide, becomes blunt more quickly and breaks more easily. However, the choice is not very critical. Try a No. 2 or 1 for ordinary work, and No. 3/0 or 4/0 for fine work. The important thing is that the spacing of the teeth should be such that the thickness of the sheet being cut will cover at least two teeth. If it it less, then the metal is liable to jam between two teeth and the blade will probably break.

To fix the blade, loosen the clamping screw at each end of the frame, insert the blade in the handle end and tighten the screw, making sure that the other end of the blade is in line with the top clamp. The teeth should point outward from the frame and downward. Brace the top of the frame against the bench, pressing fairly hard against it, insert the top end of the blade into its clamp and tighten up. When pressure on the frame is now released, the blade should be held absolutely taut.

The piece to be cut is held with one hand on or against the bench-pin, whilst the other hand works the saw vertically up and down and in a forward direction. This hand is therefore beneath the bench-pin, which means, for comfort, that one's chair or stool should be low, with the bench-pin roughly at chest level.

Holding the work-piece firmly is important: a slip will twist the blade in its frame and may snap it. If the piece is fair-sized it is placed on the bench-pin with the end which is to be cut projecting over an edge, and the fingers can then close round it and the pin like a clamp. Very small pieces, too small to hold without risk of sawing one's fingers, are best gripped in a hand vice or clamp (*12, 13*), which is then held on the bench-pin. Awkward shaped pieces are pressed against the forward edge of the pin,

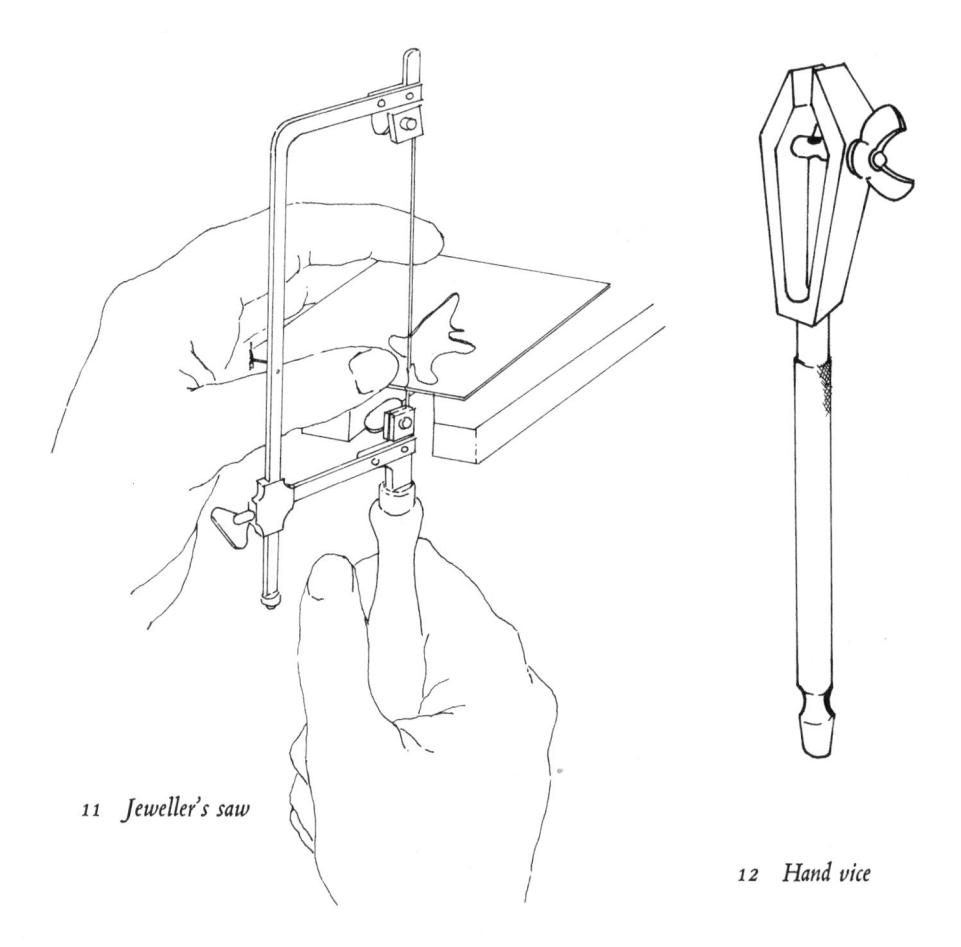

11  *Jeweller's saw*

12  *Hand vice*

in a small, V-shaped notch cut as required with the saw: a craftsman's bench-pin will look as if it had been gnawed by rats. In all cases the object is to use the bench-pin as firm base, on or against which the work-piece rests; for if this is simply held between the fingers there is bound to be movement—and blade breakage.

A cut is best started by a few upward strokes which will make a slight nick sufficient to prevent the blade from slipping about on the edge and perhaps starting to cut in the wrong place. But the actual cutting is always done on the downstroke, necessarily so because the teeth point downward. No forward pressure should be applied: the blade is merely allowed to rest against the work and pulled down or pushed up, and the more rhythmic the movement, the cleaner the line and the less risk of the blade straying and wandering about.

Inevitably the blade will sometimes jam in the cut; and if then forced will break. This is particularly liable to happen if the saw is not held vertical. Ease it out by moving it up gently and at the same time drawing it back. If this does not work,

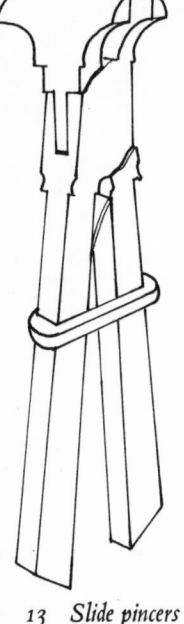

13  *Slide pincers
or clamp*

release tension on the blade by undoing the bottom clamp and push the frame up until the blade is clear.

To cut a curve, turn the metal slowly while still keeping the saw blade moving straight forward. The frame should always be in line with your shoulder. Turning it away in order to turn the blade results in loss of control over the line and, frequently, in breakage. The breakage, of course, happens because the blade has no room to turn in its cut; it will therefore become twisted if the frame is moved out of line—and a very small twist is often too much because the blade is under tension. If, on the other hand, it is the work-piece which is turned, then the blade can cut in line with the change in direction, provided the turn is not forced but keeps pace with the progress of the saw.

This principle is observed even when cutting out an angle, but here the saw, still moving up and down, is kept 'marking time' without any forward pressure at all while the sheet of metal is turned slowly until the new line of cut is reached. This process does result in a slight softening of the angle. If the design calls for a V-shaped cut ending in a sharp point, this is achieved by cutting one side, then starting afresh on the other side so that the two cuts ultimately meet.

There is an exception to the principle of holding the saw vertical and with the frame in line with the shoulder. This is when cutting out the claws of a coronet or similar stone setting in which the metal at the base between the claws is bevelled off. Here the piece itself is held at an angle to the bench, and so too, therefore, is the saw. The blade itself will still be at right angles to the work, but in order to cut the bevelled curve, the frame will have to be laid over gradually as the cutting proceeds until the centre line has been reached. The process is then repeated from the other side until the two cuts meet, freeing the waste metal.

This method of working, which may also be suitable in other cases when a solid piece of metal is being so to speak carved out, needs more skill and practice than straightforward cutting. The blade is more difficult to control, mainly because the weight of the frame is over to one side and tends to twist it, so that breakages are not infrequent, at any rate in the early stages of one's experience.

Cutting holes is a process known as *piercing*, and the first step is to drill a small hole somewhere convenient in the area which is to be cut out. A $\frac{1}{16}$ inch drill will do, but the size of the hole does not matter provided it is no smaller than the width of the sawblade.

The drawing (14) shows the traditional jeweller's drill-stock, a steel rod with a handle attached by a length of string so that it can move up and down, a heavy brass wheel near the bottom, and a chuck to hold the drill. In use the string is twisted

30

round the rod, which brings the handle near the top. The handle is then pressed down with one hand, which unwinds the string and forces the rod to turn. The weighted wheel, which is really a fly/wheel, continues to turn after the string has become unwound, and so winds it up again. The hand allows the handle to rise, then presses it down again as soon as it is at the top. The rod must be kept vertical with the drill, assisted by the weight of the hand, bearing down on the metal. The advantage of the drill/stock is that it leaves one hand free to hold the work/piece in position.

Before applying the drill, mark the place where it is to go, preferably with a centre/punch, but twisting

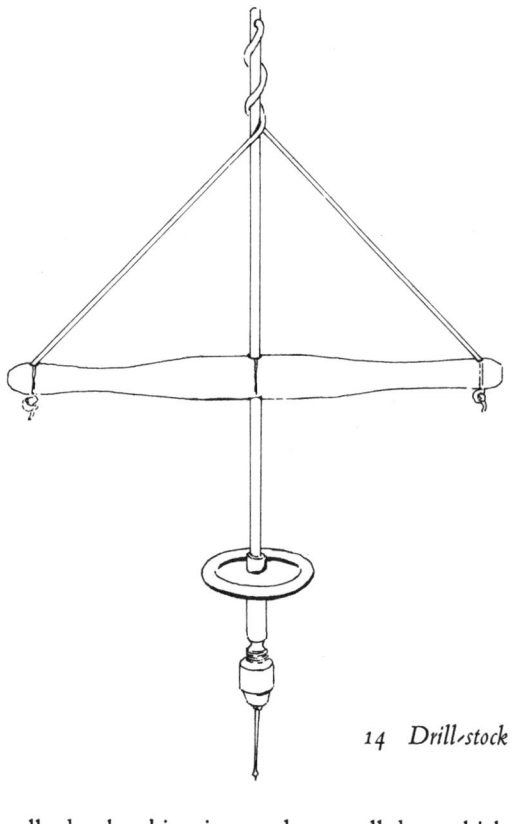

14 *Drill/stock*

the point of a scriber on it will usually do: the object is to make a small dent which will prevent the drill from straying and scratching the surface of the metal.

Next, the sawblade is released from the upper end of the frame and can then be threaded through the hole. The work/piece is slipped down to the handle end of the saw and left hanging while the blade is clamped back in position.

Sawing out the hole is done in the normal way, and when the waste metal is free, the blade is released once more and drawn out of the work.

The beginner's first efforts will involve only cutting out simple shaped holes, round, oblong or square, triangular. It is worth looking at the escapement plates of watches of the mid/nineteenth century and earlier—all hand/cut and engraved—to see what miracles of delicacy in piercing and fretting can be achieved with the simple jeweller's saw. Modern jewelry does not often call for such elaborate arabesques, but neither need it be limited in its decoration to the obvious plain geometric shapes. And even a fairly simple shape can be so small in scale as to call for a really high degree of skill to ensure perfect execution.

There are two further points to bear in mind:

If the design is an over-all design, such as would involve a fairly serious weakening of the structure, then the order of sawing out should be so organised as to leave the maximum amount of metal on the outer edges, so as to give support. In other words, one works more or less from the centre of the piece towards the outer edges.

Secondly, the little faults of line that are almost bound to occur may be difficult, or even impossible to clean up in the normal way, by filing; for the frettings may be so small that even the tiniest file cannot enter them. But the saw can be used, the flat of the blade being worked up and down against the faulty edge until the blemishes are completely removed. Here it is the sides of the saw-teeth, and not the cutting-edge, that do the work. This technique is very useful, and not only in pierced work, whenever an edge difficult to tackle with a file, such as a sharp angle, has to be cleaned up.

Before sawing begins, it is necessary to have some kind of design marked on the metal.

The main tools required are a steel rule, a square for setting out right angles as well as for checking the straightness of an edge, and a pair of dividers for marking out circles and arcs of a circle. The scriber is simply a length, 4 or 5 inches, of hardened steel rod about $\frac{3}{16}$ inch in diameter, with one end tapered down to a fine point. This point, as also the points of the dividers, will become blunted in use and must be sharpened from time to time on an oilstone.

For his first attempts the beginner will wish to practise straight lines, curves and circles. These are scratched direct on the metal with the scriber and dividers. When sawing be sure to keep to one side of the line and as close to it as possible: in later work this will be the waste side. In so far as the saw is allowed to stray from the line, there will be metal to be filed away, and consequently unnecessary work. But it is worse to cross the line for this is an encroachment upon the design which will then have to be modified, a thing not always possible.

More elaborate designs can be drawn free-hand with a pencil direct on the metal. Alternatively the design can be drawn on tracing paper and transferred through carbon paper, preferably after the surface of the metal has been painted with a thin covering of chinese white. In either case it is best to follow the drawing with a scriber, not only because the drawing rubs off fairly quickly as the metal is handled while being sawn, but also because the drawn lines are really too thick for accurate work.

## FILING

Files come in many shapes and sizes, and vary in 'cut' from the very coarse— 'bastard'—to those that are so fine—'dead-smooth'—that the teeth are almost invisible.

In jewelry work the file is normally used to clean up edges and moulded shapes, i.e. to correct and refine them where necessary; and to remove traces of sawing, deep scratches, excess solder, etc.

No great amount of metal is removed, and consequently it is not necessary to have the coarser files. And since the work-piece is usually small and often delicate, the big, heavy file will be out of place.

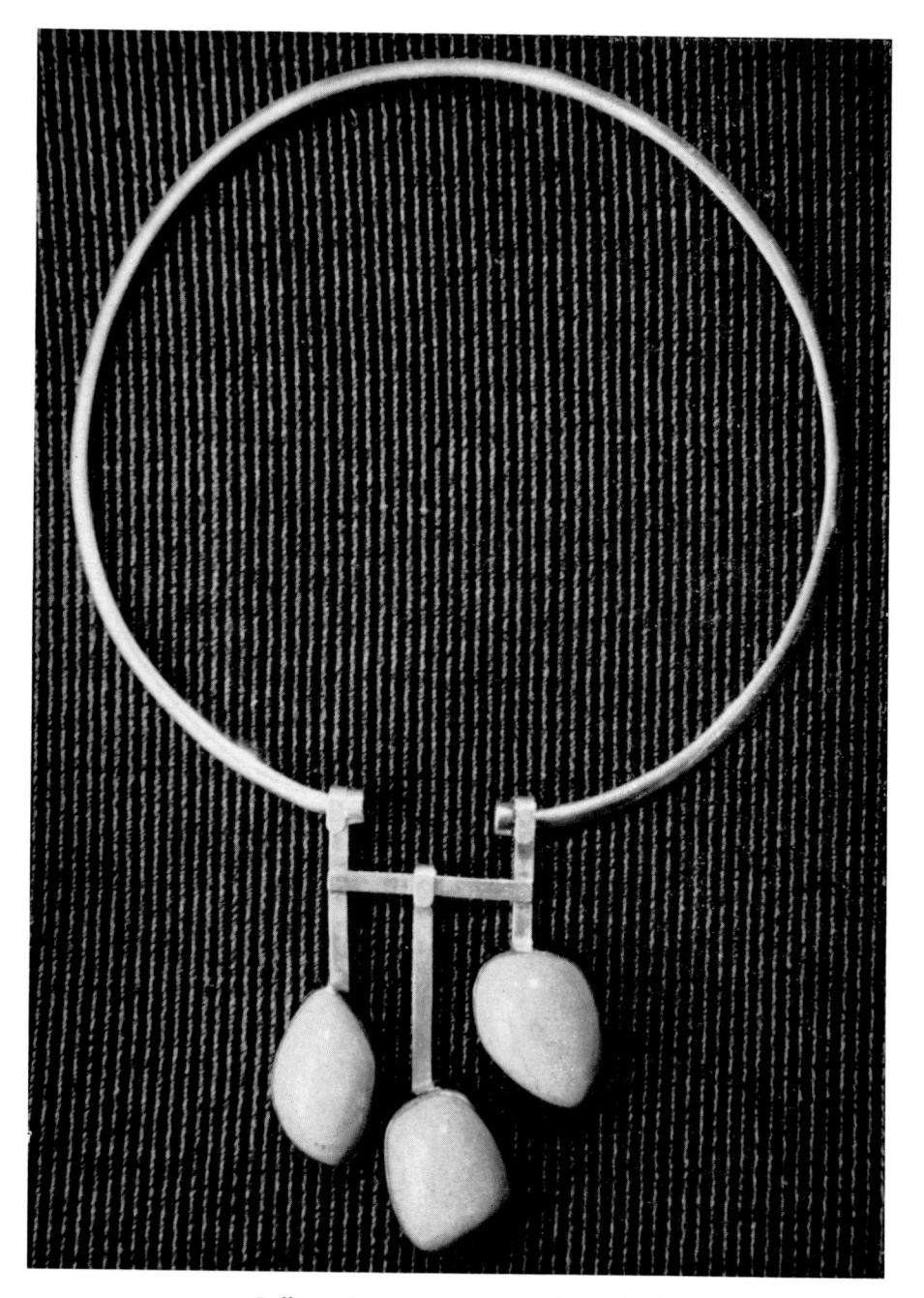

15 Collar and pendant, silver and blue cabochons

17 Ring, gold, rutilated quartz.
Double shank of flat wire

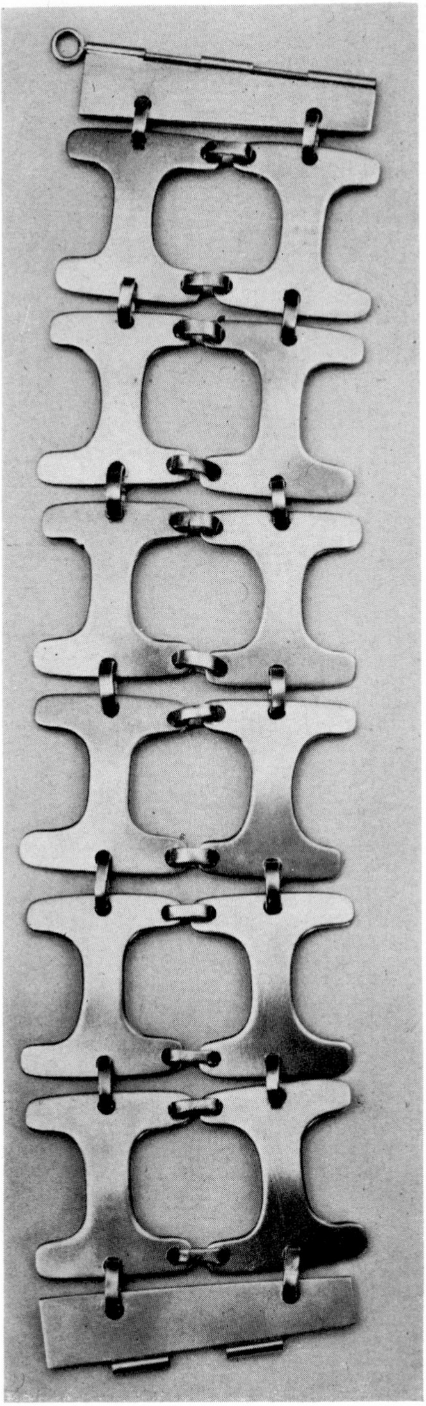

16 Bracelet in matt silver by
Helga Zahn

You will need a 6 or 8 inch hand file and half-round file, No. 2 cut and dead smooth. The hand file is a flat file, preferably with a 'safe edge', that is to say, one edge without teeth so that the inside of a right angle can be filed without risk of also filing the adjacent side. Other shapes less generally useful, but valuable on occasion, are the round file, the crossing, the square and the knife. They can be acquired as and when the need arises. All these shapes are illustrated in Chap. II(7).

For the more delicate work, the jeweller will need a selection of needle files, No. 2 cut. These files(18) are very much smaller and lighter, and unlike those already mentioned, which are made with a tang that can be driven into a wooden handle, their handles are of metal integral with the file itself. The most useful shapes here are the barrette (a flat triangle shape with two sides smooth, and therefore 'safe'), the swage, round, three-square, warding and knife. Start with the barrette, the swage, and perhaps the knife edge.

Lastly there are the specialised 'riffler' files(18), double-ended and mostly with ends curved. These are intended for deli-

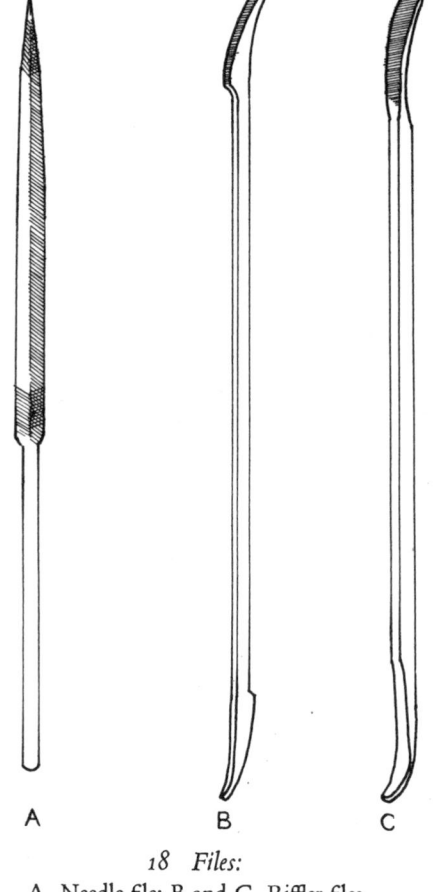

A        B        C

*18 Files:*

A. Needle file; B and C. Riffler files

cate work in fairly inaccessible places, or on concave surfaces. There must be some twenty different shapes on the market, designed to deal with the different kinds of awkwardness that can arise: they are thus best bought with a specific job in mind.

Filing is not a difficult process: but neither is it as easy as it might appear at first sight. One takes away too little, and goes on, and has then taken away too much. One takes away a high spot, and creates a fresh low spot in the process. Lines that should be straight are bumpy, and curves that should be smooth are lumpy.

The chief trouble is nervousness. There is a temptation to use files that are un-necessarily small and fine, and to scratch away with fiddly little strokes, for fear that too much metal may be removed. This is wrong. Always use the biggest file that can be applied, having regard to the size and shape of the piece, and use bold, long strokes. This is the only way to produce a firm, smooth line, free of high and low spots, with a nice clean edge, and in the shortest possible time. The proper way to control the amount of metal that is removed with each stroke is chiefly by selecting the right cut of file. If a fair amount has to be taken off, start off with your coarsest file. Finish the job with a fine one; and lastly, remove any file marks with the dead smooth file, or, if your dead smooth file is too big, finish off with carborundum paper or 'Scotch stone'.

If the line is straight, file diagonally across from one end to the other, and do not imagine that straightness can be achieved more easily by filing along the edge with the file in line with it: the latter method almost invariably results in the edge becoming sloped off either at the beginning or at the end, because it is almost impossible to maintain the same even pressure along the whole length of the file.

If the edge is curved, or has to be rounded, do not apply the file with short flat strokes in places where it seems to be needed, but let the stroke follow smoothly round the line of curve. Roll it round, so to speak, for otherwise the curve will simply develop into a series of short flats. And this principle holds good whether the curve is an outer or an inner curve.

Lastly the firm base, the bench/pin, important, if not quite as important as when sawing. If the work/piece is held in the unsupported hand, even if it is actually gripped in a hand vice, there is no means of preventing a certain amount of 'give', which will vary, or an occasional slight turn. The former means that filing pressure must be uneven, and so high spots and low spots develop. The latter means that the filed edge tilts slightly in relation to the file, and so becomes rounded and loses its sharpness. But it is one of the characteristics of a well/made piece that its planes should be well/defined, for it is these planes that flash reflected light, bringing out the beauty of the metal and giving it life.

## SOLDERING

Almost all jewelry is constructional and involves the joining together of component pieces. The design is analysed into relatively simple elements which are made separately and then soldered together. This is infinitely easier and less wasteful of material than trying to saw, file and carve the piece as a single unit out of a solid lump of metal. But soldering may even be required where we are dealing with a piece which cannot be broken down, at least not economically, into sub/units. Thus a wire formed into a chain link should have its ends soldered together for greater strength and security. A ring/shank could be sawn out of thick sheet with no great difficulty, but the piece cut out of the centre to make the opening would probably be waste which can be avoided, together with the labour of drilling, sawing and filing, by forming the shank out of suitable wire and soldering the ends together.

Soldering is achieved by bringing together the two surfaces to be joined, applying 'flux' and 'solder' to them, and heating until the solder melts and fuses into the joint.

The object of the flux is to prevent the heated surfaces becoming oxidised by contact with the air, for this would prevent the solder from adhering.

In the case of ordinary base metal work, the solder often used is a soft lead and tin alloy with a relatively low melting point which can be achieved fairly easily by the simple application of a hot soldering iron. Joints thus produced are not very elegant, however, nor particularly strong. To obtain a strong joint in an article which will have to stand up to daily wear we need a 'hard' solder. This will have a high melting point, too high to be achieved with a soldering iron, so that an intense naked flame will have to be applied by means of a blow-lamp of some kind.

Hard solders, of which there are many types, used not only in jewelry but also in engineering, are based upon silver or gold. So when we are dealing with silver or gold articles we use a silver or gold solder which ensures not only that the joint is not betrayed by a 'colour line', but also that the article is not debased by inferior metal: it remains what it claims to be, silver or gold of a particular standard.

Silver and gold solders may be obtained in sheet, strip, wire or powder form, sheet or strip being usually the most convenient to use. In the case of gold it is necessary to stipulate the degree of fineness required, according to the carat standard of the article. Silver solder conforms to sterling standard, but cheaper alloys, useful when making articles of copper, gilding metal or other base metals, are also available.

It is also necessary to specify the degree of 'hardness'. Gold solders are produced usually in three grades, hard, medium and easy. Silver solders are available in these three grades, but also as 'enamelling' (an extra hard solder used when the article is to be enamelled) and as 'extra soft'. These grades represent different melting temperatures, and the need for them becomes apparent when it is realised that the construction of an article often involves several consecutive solderings. To make a simple finger ring, for instance, mounting a stone, one would have to make a ring-shank, with the ends soldered together, another ring for the stone bezel, again with the ends soldered together, a platform on to which the bezel can be soldered, and which as a last step would itself be soldered to the shank. If the solders used all had the same melting point, then in the last stage there would be grave risk that the joints made earlier would melt and come adrift. But using different grades of solder, and starting with the hardest, their melting temperatures would not—or should not—be reached. One would therefore make the shank and bezel joints with the hard grade, join bezel to platform with medium, and platform to shank with easy.

One manufacturer gives the following melting ranges for his solders:

|  | SILVER | 9 CARAT GOLD |
|---|---|---|
| Enamelling | 730–800°C | |
| Hard | 745–778°C | 756–793°C |
| Medium | 720–765°C | 720–760°C |
| Easy | 705–723°C | 695–715°C |
| Extra easy | 680–700°C | 640–652°C |

In outward appearance the various grades are indistinguishable, but sheet gold solders, sold in standard squares weighing exactly 1 dwt, are usually stamped by the manufacturer both with the carat and the initial letter of the grade. Where there is no such mark, it is wise to scratch on your own identification.

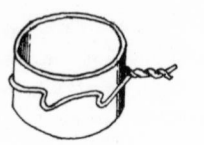

19 *Ring wired for soldering*

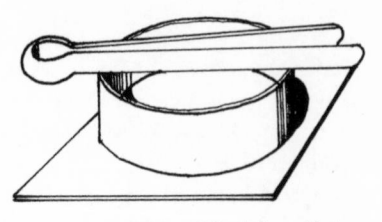

20 *Ring weighted for soldering*

## PREPARING THE WORK

Hard solders, unlike soft solders, will not fill gaps. The first step therefore is to ensure that the surfaces to be joined really fit closely together along their whole length and width. This may involve careful filing of edges, or flattening of sheet or wire by hammering it with a wooden or rawhide mallet on a steel plate. If the pieces are to be shaped by bending, and do not respond because they are work-hardened and springy, they will have to be annealed to draw their temper. Sometimes they can even be moulded into shape under heat. For instance, when it is a matter of soldering a wire to a curved surface it sometimes helps to place the wire in position, heat it gently, and while it is hot, press it carefully into close contact along its whole length: it will then keep its shape.

The next step is to ensure that the surfaces to be joined are perfectly clean. If they are greasy or dirty, then the solder will not flow or adhere properly. A freshly sawn or filed surface presents no difficulty—provided it is not fingered. Other surfaces can be lightly rubbed down with fine emery paper, or cleaned with a moist toothbrush dipped in pumice powder, and then washed under a running tap. Pieces which have been annealed should be pickled in sulphuric acid to remove oxidation.

Not only must the surfaces fit together and be clean, they may also have to be held together in place. Sometimes this is no problem. A ring-shank is usually of fairly stout material: if the ends are bent so as to overlap slightly, then drawn back and sprung into position, they will usually stay that way when the heat is applied. If not, it will have to be wired and the wire crimped to tighten it (*19*). Again, if one piece such as a decorative ring is to be soldered on to a flat surface, it can be simply laid on and may well remain in position, especially if it is fairly substantial. If it shows signs of movement as heat is applied, a steel split pin (to which the solder will not adhere) placed on top will weight it down sufficiently (*20, 21*). A light wire scroll will almost certainly move: it too should be weighted down. Moreover, particular care should have been taken to ensure that the wire is thoroughly annealed, for otherwise it will certainly twist as the metal becomes hot.

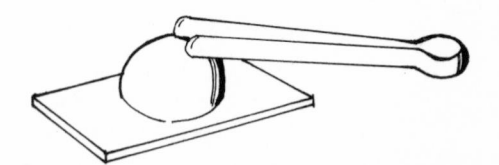

21 *Dome weighted for soldering*

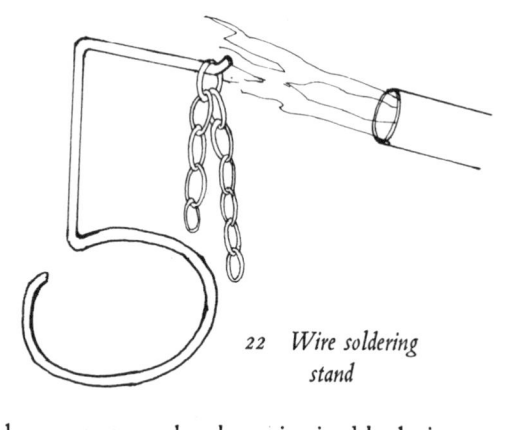

22  *Wire soldering*
*stand*

These are the simplest cases. Often, however, one has to solder together pieces which, because of their shape, will not rest conveniently one upon the other. It may be that they can be placed side by side, touching each other, as for instance when soldering together the crossbars of a T-piece, and close contact can then be maintained by laying two split pins against them.

In other cases the pieces may have to be wired or clipped together, as may be convenient. The wire used is iron binding wire, iron because with this as with the split pin, the oxide scale which forms on heating up prevents any solder from adhering permanently.

Iron wire is obtainable in all standard wire gauges. You will need a thin wire and a somewhat heavier one, say 30 S.W.G. and 22 S.W.G. (though there is nothing critical about this). The thin wire is normally used for actually binding two pieces together, a length being taken right round and the ends twisted together using pliers. If the result is too slack, as it may well be, the wire can be tightened either by crimping it in several places, again with the help of pliers, or by forming a loop and twisting this.

The thicker wire can also serve for actual binding, particularly the larger and less delicate pieces, but it tends to be somewhat stiff and less easy to manage than the thin wire. It is extremely useful, however, for forming light U-shaped clips to be used in place of split pins, and also for constructing supporting stands which are sometimes needed (22).

Every soldering problem is an individual problem, but most can be solved with the aid of simple binding wire and split pins.

## FLUXING

When metals such as iron, copper, silver and gold alloys are heated in air, the surface absorbs oxygen to form a skin of metallic oxides which prevents solder from adhering. It is therefore necessary to protect the surface from contact with the air and this is done by applying what is known as a 'flux' to the parts to be joined.

The traditional and probably still the most commonly used flux is borax in the form of a cone, though it is also available as loose crystals or a powder. A thin creamy paste is made by dissolving crystal or powder in a little water, or by rubbing the cone in water in an unglazed earthenware dish (10). The paste is painted with a small brush on and round the surfaces to be soldered. When heat is applied the flux bubbles, then dries to a white powdery deposit as the water is driven off. Heating is continued

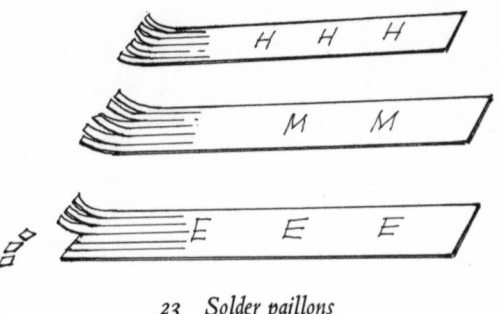

23   *Solder paillons*

until, as soldering temperature is reached, the borax melts to form a glassy skin on the joint which absorbs any oxide and prevents air from reaching the joint to form fresh oxide.

The awkward stage is the bubbling stage, for it is then that the pieces to be joined tend to lift and become displaced if they have not been adequately secured. The thinner the paste, the less the bubbling and the easier the subsequent cleaning up. Experience helps here, for the flux must not be used so meanly that it becomes burnt and useless before soldering is complete. The principle is that a very thin, watery paste is adequate where the metal is light and quickly brought to soldering temperature. With heavier pieces which need longer heating a thicker paste, about the consistency of top milk, is needed.

There are special fluxes on the market, in powder or ready-to-use liquid form, which bubble noticeably less than does borax. They are handy, but a little more expensive, and certainly less reliable than borax for the heavier joints, because they do not sustain so well the longer periods of heating involved.

## APPLYING THE SOLDER

In jewelry work, where joints are usually quite small, the solder is applied in tiny pieces known as 'paillons'. Take the strip of solder, make a series of parallel cuts with the shears, and a cut across will then produce several little snippets which ought to be roughly $\frac{1}{32}$ or $\frac{1}{16}$ inch square (23). These can be picked up one at a time with the paintbrush dipped in flux (which, of course, fluxes the solder at the same time), and one or more placed on or against the joint, depending on its length (24). One can be fairly miserly about this: if not enough to fill the joint has been applied, more can be added; but if there is too much, the excess will have to be filed off, which is a much more tedious job.

After the paillons have been applied, the next step is to heat. With a butane or propane blowpipe there is no problem, for the

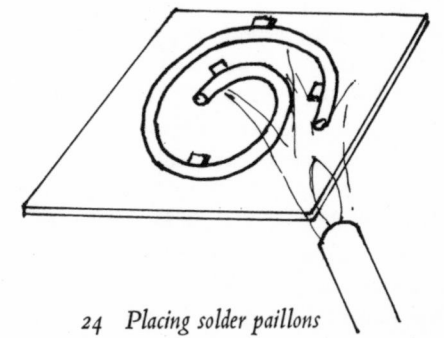

24   *Placing solder paillons*

only control is a tap which regulates the size of the flame. With a mouth blowpipe using ordinary town gas the matter is a little more complicated and needs practice. The blowpipe is fitted with two rubber tubes, one of which, the larger, is attached to the gas supply. The end of the other, usually fitted with a bone or plastic mouth-piece, is gripped between the teeth. Blowing through this carries oxygen to the flame and causes it to burn with greater intensity, though the size of the flame is still controlled by the gas tap on the blowpipe handpiece. Blowing is controlled by the cheeks, which act in effect like bellows. With experience it is possible to sustain a steady flow of air while still breathing almost normally through the nose.

It will also be noted that one can produce different types of flame, and this depends upon the amount of air supplied. The illustration (25) shows (A) a flame with insufficient air, a 'reducing' flame showing a great deal of yellow, which will probably not be hot enough and may dirty the joint with soot. The second flame (B), an 'oxidising' flame, with a long light-blue base cone is hard and dangerously hot. It may prevent the solder from flowing by oxidising the metal, and carries a strong risk that the metal will become too hot and melt. The flame shown at (C) is just right; it is mainly dark-blue, just tipped with yellow and it should be played upon the work in such a way that the light-blue base cone does not quite reach it, for the hottest part of the flame is just in front of this.

All this suggests that the mouth blow-pipe is one to be avoided. This is not so. It is much easier to handle than the

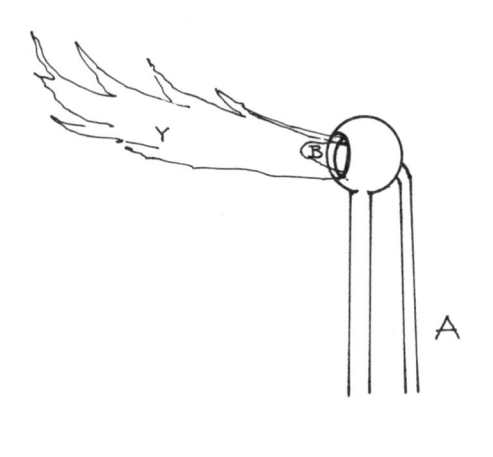

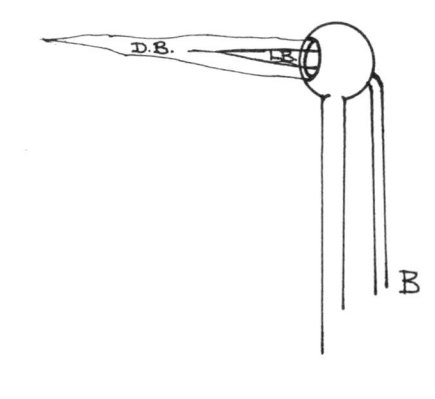

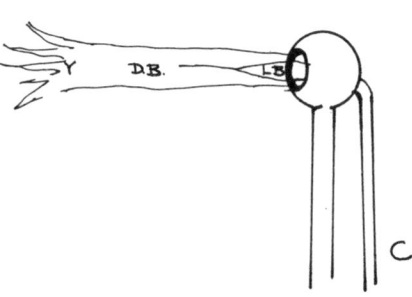

25  *Types of flame*

A. Reducing; B. Oxidising; C. Soldering. Colours: Y, yellow; B, blue; LB, light-blue; DB, dark-blue

description makes it seem, and above all the intensity of the flame can be controlled and varied much more quickly and easily than with any other type of equipment. But it does need practice until the trick of it is caught.

Now to solder. Place the work-piece on an asbestos or charcoal block. Begin with a soft, gentle flame, playing it over the whole piece so as to warm it up gradually and evenly. This is important because uneven heating may result in distortion. During this preliminary heating the flux will bubble. Watch the joint for signs of movement: if you like, take away the flame when all bubbling has stopped, inspect carefully and re-adjust if necessary. It is useful, incidentally, to have a pair of steel tweezers at hand— or even to hold them—ready for immediate action, or to enable you to pick up the work-piece in order to inspect it from different angles while actually soldering. Steel and not brass, incidentally, because there is no risk of melting them in the flame, nor will they become soldered to the work-piece as might happen with brass tweezers.

When satisfied that everything is in order, increase the flame and bring the metal to soldering temperature as quickly as possible. This temperature is reached when the metal begins to turn a very dark, dull red, and this is most easily judged if the soldering is done in subdued light. Simultaneously the solder melts and runs, filling in the joint, a process known as 'flushing'. It is quite unmistakable, for the solder shows up as a very bright streak.

From this description it is apparent that the solder should not be heated directly by the flame, but indirectly by heat conduction from the metal. If the solder is heated directly by the flame, it will, of course, melt just as well, but the chances are that it will not flow, because the metal, being larger than the solder paillon, will not reach soldering temperature as quickly as the solder.

A similar point comes up in connection with the work-piece itself when two or more components are being joined. Here almost always one piece is smaller than the other, and will heat up more quickly even if the flame is played equally upon both. In these conditions there is the risk that it will actually reach its melting-point before the larger piece is hot enough to solder, and the only way to guard against this is to concentrate the flame upon the main component and rely upon conductivity to heat up the smaller component. In the case of silver and gold the danger sign appears when the metal becomes bright red: almost immediately after a kind of shimmer appears on its surface, which means that the outer skin has begun to melt. Always watch out for this and shift the flame the moment it appears, or you think it may appear, for it is only a flash from here to the next stage, which is complete collapse of the piece.

Some idea of the risk may be obtained from a comparison of the melting temperatures of solders given on p. 37 with those of silver and gold, which are 780–890°C for sterling, and 820–1310°C for gold, depending on alloy and carat. The margin is obviously small, especially in the case of enamelling solder. And so there is one point to be made, and two rules to be remembered. Have your inevitable accident early, and learn from it. Never take your eyes off the point of the flame, for that is where the danger lies. Remember that the lighter the piece, the more quickly it heats up.

42

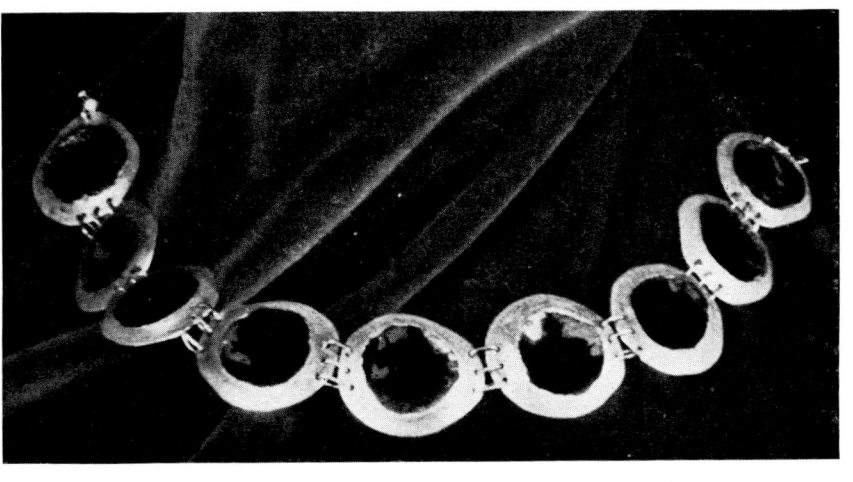

26 Necklace in copper, silver-plated with blue and green enamels. Centre of links hollowed with a large rounded punch to form recess for the enamel

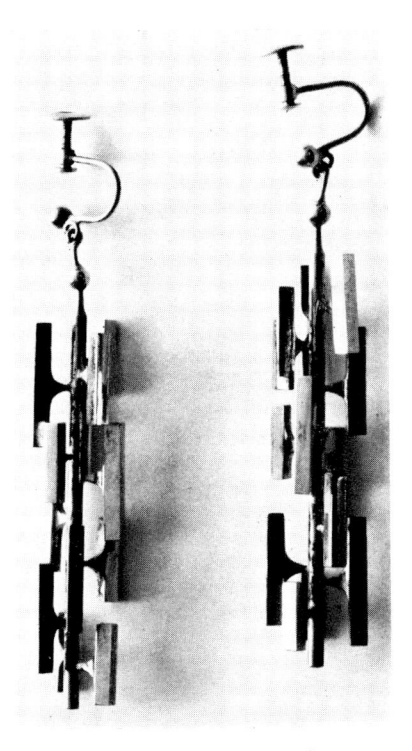

27 Ring, gold, smoky quartz

28 Silver gilt earrings by David Thomas

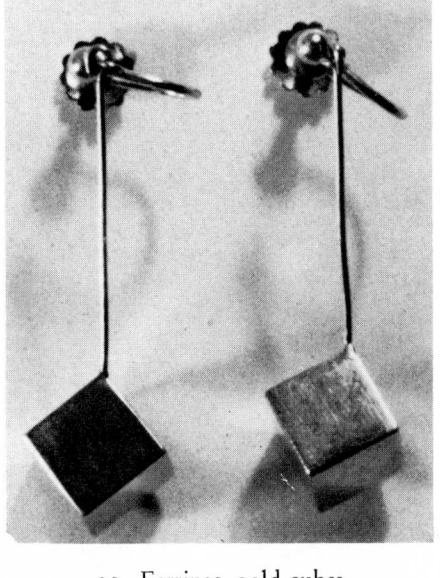

29  Gold brooch by John Donald

31  Ring, silver, cabochon amethyst. The base of the setting was formed with a punch filed to repeat the shape of the stone

30  Earrings, gold cubes

The molten solder runs, and it always runs towards the hotter part of the metal. This characteristic is very useful. It enables us to 'draw' the solder along the joint, merely by moving the flame along it. It also enables us to draw it right through the joint, thus making sure that it is well filled, simply by applying the flame on the opposite side and watching for the solder to flush through towards the flame. This point is illustrated (*32*).

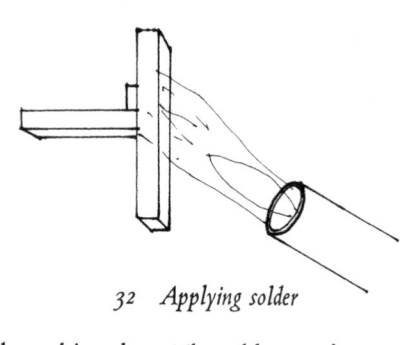

*32   Applying solder*

Normally everything goes well: occasionally nothing does. The solder won't run. It may just melt into a ball. A part of the joint may solder, and the rest won't. The answer is always either dirt or incomplete or uneven heating. The latter cause will disappear if one continues to heat all round the joint. The former means starting again from the beginning, by pickling the work-piece in hot acid (having first removed any iron binding wire or clips), washing, re-fluxing and re-assembling.

When soldering is complete, the work-piece should be pickled in sulphuric acid gently warmed up to remove the deposit of flux and the oxide which will have formed on unfluxed surfaces. Before this is done any binding wire, etc., should be removed, for this reacts chemically to produce unpleasant stains on the work-piece. For this reason, too, the work-piece should be placed into and taken out of the acid only with brass tweezers which do not produce this reaction. When pickling is complete, the work-piece is washed and is then ready for the next step.

## FINISHING OFF

Finishing-off is the last basic step in jewelry making and consists in removing all scratches, dents and other surface blemishes, and applying the final finish, which may be a high polish, or a matt texturing or even a surface colouring. All this can involve a great deal of work and it is as well to anticipate the need for it and do it so far as possible as one goes along.

This means that each component piece should be inspected when finished, scratches, excess solder, etc., cleaned up, and the piece polished up. The reason for doing the work at the component stage is that it is much more easily done with a single component than with the final assembly since this is necessarily more complex in shape and may well have inaccessible parts. To take an obvious example, you can, of course, polish a complete T-piece: but you will then find that it is quite a problem to clean up the angles without spoiling their proper hard line. If, however, the two arms are polished separately before being soldered together, then all that may be needed to finish off at the end is a simple rub to restore the polish.

The principle in finishing off is to start by tackling the worst marks with a medium abrasive or file, following successively with finer abrasives until the finest is reached for the final polish. Obviously, however, it is pointless to start with a medium file if the only marks to be dealt with are light superficial scratches; and a waste of time to start with a fine abrasive if the marks are deep.

There are many abrasives on the market. Those most commonly used are emery paper in various grades of fineness, Water-of-Ayr stone, tripoli usually in cake form, rouge both in cake and powder form, and whiting powder (which some prefer to rouge powder because it is not so messy).

Excess solder and deep scratches usually need a file to remove them. A medium, or even a fine file, straight or rounded according to the shape of the piece, should suffice. Except when actually working in a corner, the filing action should be taken beyond the actual mark being removed and faded out gradually in order not to create a fresh and worse mark. A scratch in a concave surface can probably be treated with a suitably curved riffler file, or alternatively with a strip of fine emery paper folded into a small pad. Emery paper can also be used on flat and convex surfaces, but one has to be careful when working near edges not to round these off, unless, of course, they are intended to be rounded. To preserve flatness it often helps to wind the emery paper round a flat file, for in this way it is possible to apply the paper with an even pressure over the whole surface.

After the coarser scratches have been removed there will still remain fine scratches, sometimes so fine as to be invisible to the eye, but still sufficient to prevent a good polish. These are removed with Water-of-Ayr stone, a very soft, slate-like stone obtainable in square section sticks. One-eighth and $\frac{1}{4}$ inch sticks are useful sizes, and one should use the biggest size that can conveniently be applied. If there are awkward corners to be reached, the end of the stick can be pointed by rubbing down on coarse emery paper. Dip one end of the stick into water and commence rubbing the surface, working either in one direction only or with a circular motion on the larger surfaces. The stick should be kept well wetted, and as with the file and the emery paper, one must be careful not to concentrate so much on one spot that depressions and flats develop.

Just as emery paper is an alternative, less satisfactory but sometimes unavoidable, to the file, so there is an alternative to the Water-of-Ayr stone in the form of a very fine paper known as tripoli paper, this being the abrasive it carries. The disadvantage is the same as with emery paper, the risk of applying it with uneven pressure so as to produce an uneven surface, the risk of rounding off edges and planes which should be hard. But it can be extremely useful, especially in hard-to-get-at corners.

The work should be washed and inspected fairly often. When it presents an absolutely even matt surface, it is ready for the final polish. For this we use jeweller's rouge either in cake form (when it is compounded with a hard grease as a binder) or in powder form mixed to a paste with water. The rouge is applied with a cloth or a chamois leather rubbed quite hard on smooth surfaces, or with a stiffish brush—an old toothbrush will do very well—where the surface is decorated and full of small, hard-to-get-at crannies and recesses. Sometimes where the part is especially awkward to reach, it may be necessary to apply the rouge with an orange stick.

The sides of holes pierced or formed in the surface are most conveniently dealt with by 'threading': tie a few short lengths of linen thread (special thread for the purpose can be bought in hanks) to a nail driven into the side of the work-bench, pull them taut with one hand and rub the cake of rouge on them in order to cover them with abrasive, then pass a convenient number of threads through the hole and draw the work-piece to and fro until the sides of the hole are polished. Keep the threads as taut as possible when working on straight sides, and watch that these do not become rounded. Be particularly careful to work evenly over the whole surface and never to stay on one point, for a thread is quick to cut a groove where no groove should be.

The last step is to wash the article in warm water with a little detergent, and using a soft brush to remove all traces of rouge and grease.

What we have described is polishing by hand methods. Quicker results can be achieved if one has access to an electric motor and polishing buffs, though even here some of the work will have to be done by hand. Deep scratches, for instance, are still best removed with a file; and excess solder in a joint cannot be removed in any other way, unless one is prepared to polish off a good deal of the metal as well. Very delicate pieces would be too much at risk, and should not be offered to a polishing wheel at all.

The motor (33) is a fractional horse-power motor, $\frac{1}{10}$ h.p. will suffice, with preferably a speed of not less than 2,800 r.p.m. The shaft should be fitted with a threaded taper (known as a 'false nose') on to which the polishing wheels can be screwed. False noses are available either with a left-hand or a right-hand thread, the choice depending on whether the shaft is on the left or right of the motor. If the wrong thread is used, then the polishing wheel will become unscrewed in use because the pressure applied acts as a brake on the wheel, tending to slow it down in relation to the shaft. The buffs, 4–6 inches diameter, should consist of a felt wheel for plain surfaces, a hard and a soft brush for complicated surfaces, a medium and a soft (swansdown) calico buff for most surfaces.

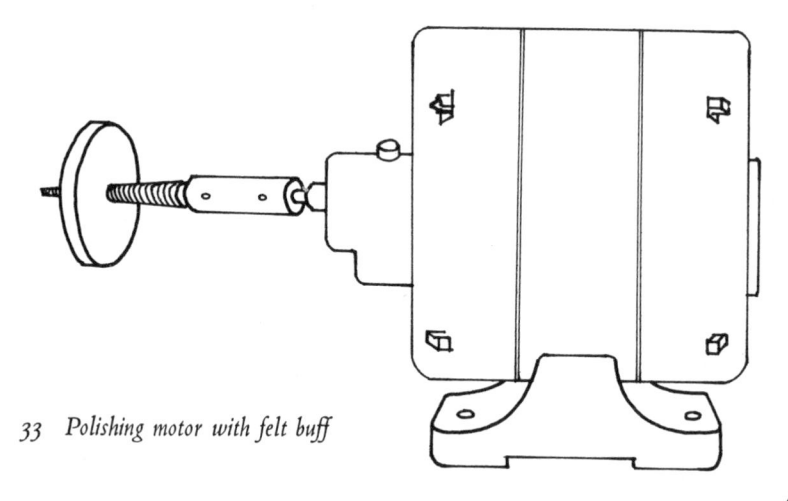

*33  Polishing motor with felt buff*

The abrasives used are tripoli and rouge, both in cake form. The tripoli serves on all the buffs other than the soft brush and the swansdown which are used with rouge for the final polish.

The operator stands in front of the motor with the wheel spinning towards him from the top. The mop is charged by holding the cake against it while it is turning. The work-piece is held touching the edge of the mop near the bottom.

There are two risks to guard against. The first, more serious, is that the wheel may catch the work-piece, spin it out of your hands and probably damage it. This may happen if too much pressure is applied, or, very easily, if when polishing an edge, the piece is held so that the edge points upwards against the direction of rotation. It is also liable to happen with chain which, being flexible, tends to curl round the wheel; chain can only be handled safely if it is stretched on a piece of wood, if necessary a section at a time, and so offered up to the wheel with any loose ends, of course, held out of harm's way.

The second risk is the same as with hand-polishing, the risk of achieving unwanted effects by over-concentration on one spot: only it materialises much more quickly because the wheel is so much faster working. Consequently the work-piece has to be kept moving, with fresh surfaces constantly being offered up to prevent flats and hollows from developing, hard edges being softened and so on.

Wheels become clogged in time. They can be cleaned quite easily by holding the edge of a large file against them for a few seconds while spinning. A dirty wheel shows itself by building up black, greasy deposits on the work-piece: but this can also happen if the wheel is not turning at sufficient speed. In such a case the answer is not a different motor, but a larger buff; for what matters is not so much the speed of the motor as the peripheral speed of the buff, and this for any given speed of motor increases as the size of the wheel increases.

After all polishing has been done, the work should be scrubbed with a soft nail-brush in warm water and detergent to remove all traces of grease and then dried. Usually nothing further is needed, but sometimes a special finish may be desired, and this can now be applied.

## MATT FINISHES

In the trade a usual method of producing a matt finish is by sandblasting, which involves blowing a jet of compressed air carrying a fine grit on to the surfaces to be treated. This results in an even pitting of the area, which produces the matt effect, and it can be varied by the use of different sizes of grit. The equipment needed is unfortunately rather expensive, but a professional polisher will do the work quite cheaply.

Different effects can be achieved by rubbing the work with a small pad of fine steel wool or a file. The important thing here is to rub or file in one direction only, so as to produce a series of fine parallel scratches. Again, the effect can be varied, this time by using different grades of steel wool and varying the pressure with which it is applied.

48

With this method, as with the other surface treatments to be described, it pays to experiment before operating on a finished piece, for without experience it is impossible to visualise exactly what the effect will be. Fortunately mistakes can usually be cured, but only by a complete re-polish.

An alternative to the wire wool, if you have a polishing motor, is to use a wire brush wheel. Such wheels are available either with steel or brass wire, and in different grades of coarseness and hardness. Choose a fairly fine and soft one, brass being the best for all metals other than silver, which tends to become yellowish through deposit of brass.

The work should only just touch the wheel, with no pressure behind it, and as with the wire wool, the treatment should be applied in one direction only.

## COLOURING METALS

Striking results can be produced on copper, brass and to a lesser extent on silver articles by colouring their surfaces. The methods are chemical, employing different formulae. They should be used with discretion, and except with black very seldom to produce a single colour overall: subtle toning, relieved by high lights, is rather the effect to be sought, and this is the more sensible since colouring will wear off in use and high lights will therefore tend to develop in any case on projecting surfaces.

The article to be treated must be absolutely clean. This is best achieved by a preliminary scouring with a damp toothbrush dipped in pumice powder, then rinse under a tap to get rid of all pumice.

Some of the formulae given are used cold, and with these it is possible to apply the chemical only on isolated areas, using a twist of cotton wool on the end of a matchstick. Others have to be used hot, and here it may be necessary to dip the whole article.

In either case the article is rinsed after the required depth of colour has been reached, and high lights and gradations of colour are then developed by rubbing with moist fine pumice powder followed by a paste of whiting. This can be done using a small damp cloth pad: but the index finger is better for the purpose since it allows better control.

1 *Copper*

(i) BRIGHT PURPLE-RED

Heat to red heat and drop in boiling water. The colouring produced is a mottled purple-red, unpredictable and often very exciting.

(ii) BROWN

| Solution: | Copper sulphate | 1 part |
|---|---|---|
| | Water | 2 parts |

Scour the article thoroughly with pumice, then dip in hot solution. Repeat to intensify and secure an even colouring.

(iii) 'ANTIQUE GREEN'
Solution:

| | | |
|---|---|---|
| Copper nitrate | 48 grains |
| Ammonium chloride | 48 grains |
| Calcium chloride | 20 grains |
| Water | 4 fluid ounces |

Immerse for several days until the desired shade is reached, then dry. Protect by brushing on a thin even film of beeswax.

If a darker green is wanted, add to the solution 10 grains of copper sulphate and 10 grains of oxalic acid.

(iv) OLIVE GREEN
Solution:

| | |
|---|---|
| Ammonium chloride | 1 part |
| Water | 2 parts |

Paint on hot and repeat to deepen the colour.

(v) BLACK
Dip in a hot, concentrated solution of barium sulphide.

## 2 Silver

(i) DARK GREY TO BLACK
Solution:

| | |
|---|---|
| Ammonium sulphide (concentrated solution) | 1 part |
| Water | 6 parts |

Ammonium sulphide is bought in lumps and should be stored in an airtight dark bottle kept away from light, in which it deteriorates. A concentrated stock solution is made up by dissolving several lumps in a half-pint of water heated almost to boiling.

Dilute the stock solution, heat almost to boiling then suspend the article in it completely using a hook made up of a length of silver wire. Dip repeatedly until the required depth and evenness of colour has been reached, then rinse.

To achieve a jet-black reduce the dilution of water added to the stock solution to two or three parts.

(ii) STEEL BLUE
Take an old tin and heat to red heat to destroy any tinning or other coating on the inside. Place the article in the tin together with two or three small lumps of sulphur (which must not touch the article), replace the lid and heat, inspecting from time to time, until the proper colour has been reached. The sulphur fumes which develop are poisonous, so do not inhale. The work should be carried out in a well-ventilated room.

(iii) REDDISH-BROWN
Solution:

| | |
|---|---|
| Barium sulphide | 10 grains |
| Water | 10 ounces |

Use cold and leave the work immersed until the desired colour has been reached.

# CHAPTER IV

## *The First Pieces*

We have described the basic processes, filing, sawing, piercing, soldering and polishing. Let us now see what we can do with them. It is quite a lot: one of the attractions of jewelry making is that it is possible with only elementary skills (but a reasonable degree of care) to make from the very start pieces that are perfectly wearable. Indeed, with ingenuity and invention one need never go beyond the basic skills, though obviously scope will be more limited.

The first example is a pure exercise, and an intensive one at that. Do it: repeat it by all means, varying the design as you wish. The other two examples are quite simple yet effective pieces of jewelry. They too exercise basic skills; but the important thing they teach is an attitude of mind, the analytical approach needed to solve a problem economically and effectively.

## FLOWER DESIGN

On a piece of sheet, 10 or 12 B.M.G., of copper, brass, or German silver, scribe a 2 inch circle with a pair of dividers. Using a protractor, measure a 72° angle at the centre and with a scriber mark the points of intersection of the two lines thus obtained where they cut the circle. Now set the dividers on the two points and scribe an arc. This gives a further point of intersection with the circle. Move the dividers to this and scribe a further arc. Repeat twice and you will have your five petals marked out. Scribe a further circle to cross the five arcs at their points of intersection, and a smaller circle inside this. This com-pletes the marking out of the flower.

Next in the spaces between the petals strike a further series of short arcs, using the points of the petals as the centres for the dividers and scribing in the space beyond the next petal: fourteen arcs will form three chevrons, a sergeant's stripes, and will complete the marking out of the design.

Now saw round the outer

34  *Flower design*

51

circle, keeping outside the line but as close as possible without actually cutting into it. Finish off by filing up to the line with a flat file, using nice long strokes following the curve, and keeping the flat of the file at right angles so as to ensure a clean crisp edge.

The next step is to pierce out the centre circle and the chevrons. Drill a small hole in each, thread the saw blade and saw round, keeping on the inside of the scribed line. Finish off by filing with needle-files, round or half-round for the centre hole, flat or barrette for the chevrons, and triangular for the corners which should be quite sharp with no trace of rounding. If the chevron holes are too small for your files, use the piercing-saw by working the flat of the blade up and down against the edges and in the corners.

We now need three rings, using round copper wire, say 18 or 20 S.W.G., one to go round the outer edge, and two in the centre. To make the rings, formers of some kind will have to be used. Store cupboard, dressing-table or medicine cupboard will probably provide a bottle, cream jar or powder box of the right diameter. For the two centre rings, a ring triblet is of course ideal, but if you have none, then again ingenuity will have to play its part, as so often in jewelry. For the centre hole a thick knitting needle or a round pencil, possibly thickened by winding round a few layers of paper, will serve. The intermediate ring could perhaps be shaped round a tube of aspirins or a round file handle.

Wind the wire round the former, mark with a file the point where the two ends overlap, remove from the former and cut through with the saw. The ends of the ring should be bent together till they overlap slightly, then brought back and sprung together so that they meet exactly. They are then soldered and pickled in sulphuric acid. By this time they will probably have lost their shape and should be slipped back on to their formers to round them up again. The rings can now be placed in position on their circles and soldered on, using a medium solder and weighting them with one or two iron split pins to prevent movement when soldering. Pickle again.

Next the petal outlines are formed, each separately using the same wire as for the rings. They can be shaped by finger pressure alone, but using flat pliers to ensure a sharp point at the ends, and should, of course, be tested from time to time by being placed on the scribed lines. When this is done satisfactorily, they are placed on top of the scribed lines and soldered on.

The final step is to stone off all scratches, scribe marks and the like, and polish.

## CUBE EARRINGS

These earrings were made of 9 carat gold sheet, 6 B.M.G. Silver will do perfectly well, or copper or any of the base metals (which, if the piece is well made, can be silver or gold plated subsequently).

A cube is a six-sided figure which can be cut and opened up to form a flat T-piece (*39* A). Mark out two such pieces with scriber and square, using the dividers to make certain that the sides of all the squares scribed are equal. The length of the sides is a

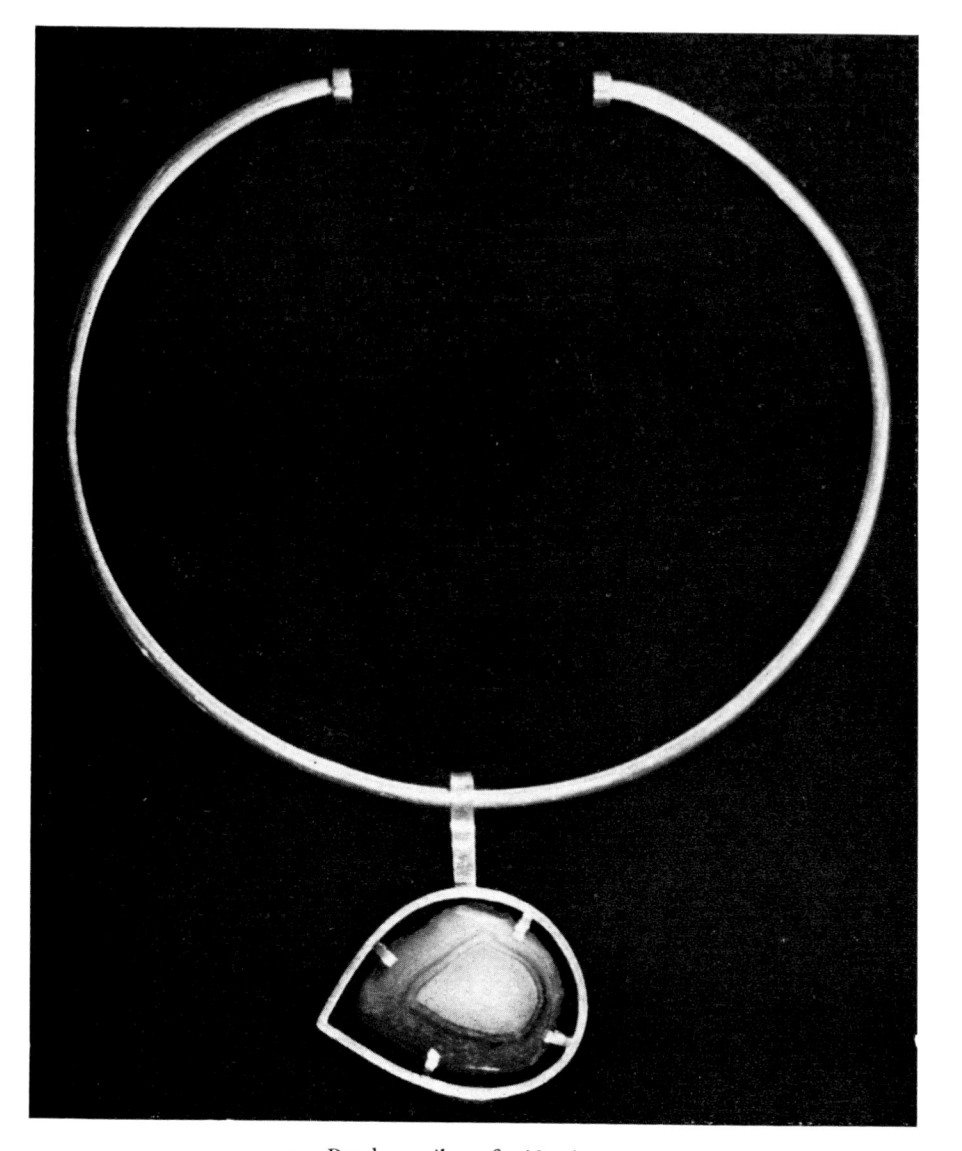

35  Pendant, silver, fortification agate

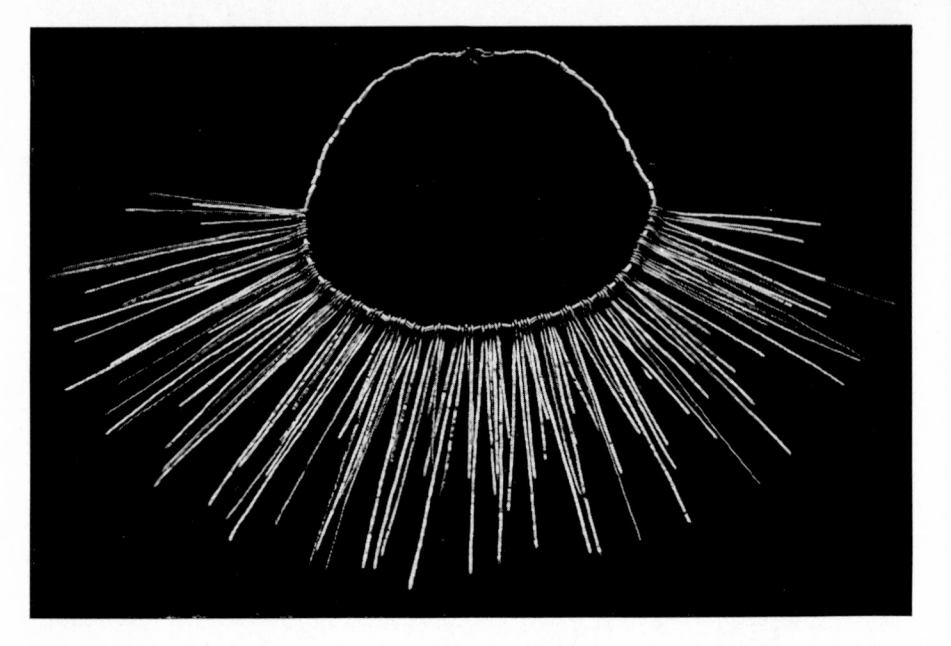

36  Necklace in hammered silver wire by Michelle Connolly

37  Ring, silver, green cabochon tourmaline

38  Ring, silver and turquoise

matter of taste. In the example shown in the photograph (*30*) they are 8 mm.

Saw out each piece as one unit, and file a 45° bevel all round; these bevels are needed to enable the cut sides to meet in a neat joint.

There will be left uncut five sides which will have to be bent up to form right angles. To enable this to be done file V-shaped grooves along the scribed lines, using the corner of a square needle-file. These grooves are the equivalent of the bevels on the outer edges and they should be taken to a depth just short of cutting through the material (*39* B). Looking ahead now to the time when a wire will have to be soldered to the cube, file off just the tip of the corner at (*a*) and with the square or a triangular file make a small nick in what will be the corresponding corner at (*b*).

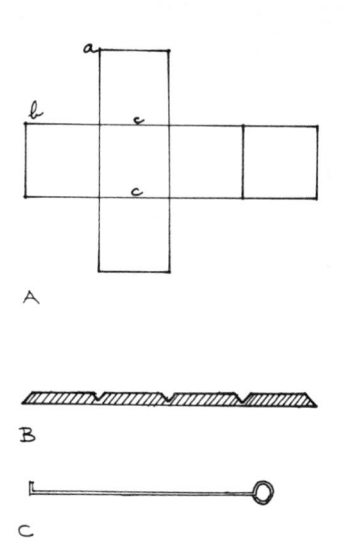

39   Cube earrings

Now anneal the piece, pickle and wash. The object of the annealing is to enable the sides of the cube to be bent up without undue risk of the material breaking at the filed edges where it is thin. Even so, care will be needed.

The cube is soldered in two stages. Bend the centre piece to shape, if necessary using the square to make sure that the angles are right angles, borax the joints (three inner filed edges and one open edge) and solder with hard grade solder. Pickle again and wash, borax the two remaining filed edges and bend up the sides to complete the cube. Borax the open edges and solder all round with medium solder, being careful at the end to bring the two filed edges at (*c*) to soldering heat so as to draw solder into the joint from the adjacent sides.

The cube is now complete save for its wire (*39* C), for which we have left a small hole. The wire used was 23 S.W.G. round which happened to be available. One or two sizes thicker would have done perfectly well. If a base metal is used it should be German silver or brass, copper being too soft. Two lengths of about $1\frac{1}{4}$ inch will be needed (this is a matter of taste). About $\frac{1}{16}$ inch at one end is bent over into an angle, and the other end is formed into a tiny ring. If the hole in the cube is too small for the wire, enlarge it by inserting the point of a round needle-file and twisting it round. Borax the hole and the angled end of the wire; insert the latter and solder with soft solder. The easiest way to do this is to hold up the ring end of the wire with tweezers so that the cube hangs free and the turned over end of the wire lies along inside one of the cube edges.

Pickle, wash and polish. The cube is now ready to attach to an ear screw; for pierced ears the attached wire can itself be formed into a hook instead of a ring.

# AGATE PENDANT(35)

It is often possible to find odd-shaped stones in junk-shops, or at dealers in semi-precious stones or mineral specimens: and they can be quite inexpensive. The stone in the pendant is one of these finds, a slice of fortification agate (the name comes from the pattern of lines which suggests the walls of a medieval fortified town) polished front and back as a mineral specimen and with the edges left rough.

The shape of the stone suggested the design, a surround (40 A) bent up from silver rectangular wire $\frac{1}{8}$ inch wide by $\frac{1}{16}$ inch thick, the ends bevelled off to meet in a joint which, if neatly soldered, will be quite invisible.

Polish the outer ring when made, and wash off all traces of grease in warm water and detergent.

The claws are four strips of 12 B.M.G. sheet cut $\frac{1}{16}$ inch wide, or flat wire. The length of the strips depends on the spacing between outer ring and stone, and on the thickness of the stone. It is as well to make them generously long: any excess can be filed off when the claws are in position and can be tested with the stone dropped in loose. Approximately one-third of each strip should be bent to a right angle upon which the stone will rest (B). The outer ring is boraxed where the claws are to be fixed, and placed on a charcoal or asbestos block. The backs of the claws, too, are boraxed and they are placed in position, touching the ring. They should stand quite easily, but if any difficulty is experienced, make up small clips of iron wire to hold them.

When the claws have been soldered, the stone should be tested for fit: if there is clearance between its edges and the claws, this can be taken up by soldering in small blocks cut from scrap pieces of metal (C). Pickle and wash as usual, then polish.

The next step is to make a kind of shepherd's crook (D) of 12 B.M.G. strip, $\frac{1}{8}$ inch wide or a little more. The hook must be sufficiently big to hook on to the silver collar from which it will hang. The end of the hook should be neatly bevelled, the other end filed to a slight concave curve which should fit the edge of the ring exactly.

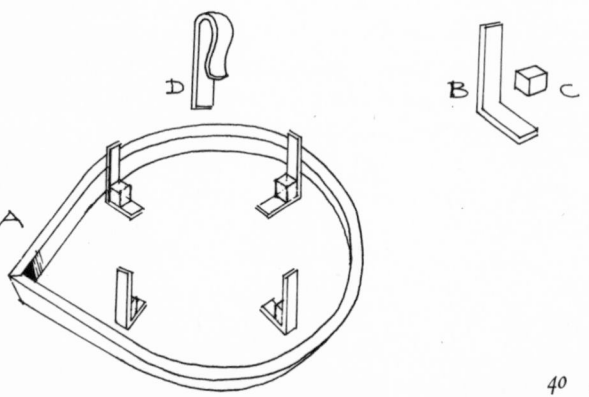

40   *Agate pendant*

Ring and hook are laid together on the charcoal block and soldered. Pickle and re‑polish all over, not forgetting to remove any excess solder.

The stone is placed in position and the tops of the claws are carefully bent over with flat pliers until the stone is gripped firmly, with no suspicion of movement. Lastly, the tips of the claws are bevelled off and any marks left by the pliers removed with a dead smooth file. Re‑polish if necessary.

The collar—which can serve for a whole range of pendants—is a $15$ inch length of half‑round wire, $\frac{5}{32}$ inch wide by $\frac{1}{16}$ inch thick which is bent by hand into a circle, leaving a gap of approximately $1$ inch at the ends. A kitchen jar will provide the necessary former. The bending should be done on the edge, not on the flat of the wire, steadily and carefully, so as to produce a nice smooth ring. You will not find it possible to keep the ring entirely flat, but the slight twist that is bound to develop will ensure that the flat rests snugly on the neck. In any case do not anneal, since the collar needs to be as springy as possible.

The ends are then filed square and 'buttons', slices $\frac{1}{8}$ inch thick cut from $\frac{1}{4}$ inch square rod, soldered on. The easiest way to do this is to prop the circle on edge with the end to be soldered resting on the button which is laid flat on the charcoal block. In this way it is possible so to arrange the position that one edge of the button is parallel with the flat of the ring and overlaps it by about $\frac{1}{32}$ inch, with, of course, a bigger overlap at the top and sides. When soldered and pickled, the buttons can be filed to repeat the half‑round shape of the wire. Lastly, polish.

In use the collar will tend to become slightly distorted, since it has to be sprung open to fit on to the neck: but this can be corrected from time to time, and the tendency will gradually disappear, as the metal hardens up with constant springing open and re‑closing.

# CHAPTER V

## Stone Settings

Most jewelry features stones, for stones are one of the easiest ways of introducing vivid touches into one's personal colour scheme, and nature, fortunately, has created a vast palette in its minerals.

The jewelry trade is primarily concerned with cut stones, of which the oldest form is the *cabochon*. This cut is applied to opaque and also to some transparent stones. It is regular in shape, usually round, oval or square, though there are fancy shapes such as hearts, but its essential characteristic is that the whole surface is smooth and rounded. The base is almost always flat, but sometimes concave to thin the stone and thereby lighten the colour, or convex (*double cabochon*).

The second cut is the *facet* in which the top and bottom surfaces are ground into mathematically exact flat planes which will break light into spectrum colours and are so calculated as to ensure the brightest possible refraction and reflection of light. The cabochon cut is essentially one for opaque stones, and for those transparent or translucent stones which would not be improved by being faceted. But a diamond, for instance, cut cabochon would look like a rather indifferent piece of glass: it is faceting which gives it brilliance and life. Since the reason for faceting is purely optical, dependent upon the manner in which the stone transmits light, there is obviously little point in faceting opaque stones, but in some cases it does improve reflection from the surface, and so we find it applied to such stones as jet.

For centuries cabochon and faceted stones have been the only types used in jewelry, but now the wheel has swung full circle. With *tumbled* stones and *roughs* we have returned to the time thousands of years ago when man had not yet discovered how to cut stones.

Tumbled stones are pebbles which have been rolled about in a rotating barrel containing abrasive grit. This treatment polishes the surface without altering the shape of the stone. It is essentially the same treatment as stones undergo under the action of the waves on a beach, but it achieves in a few hours and rather better a result which nature takes years to arrive at.

Roughs are—roughs: simply bits of stone of sufficiently attractive colour and shape to require no further treatment by way of cutting or polishing. Mostly they are natural crystals which 'grew' as the earth solidified and developed.

Tumbled stones can be obtained from dealers in gemstones, but are not yet as freely available in this country as they are in America. Rough stones can be bought from dealers in mineral specimens: there is a great deal of interest, however, in finding your own, and plenty are to be found in this country, though you will need a book on minerals to start you off, and your search can be arduous.

The character of the stone determines the character of the setting, and indeed of the whole piece. Faceted stones belong to formal jewelry and call for formal settings. The amateur can try his hand at this when he has reached a fairly advanced degree of skill, but in this field he can seldom hope to compete with the trade. Cabochons are much easier to set, using an ordinary bezel setting. Tumbled stones can sometimes be set in a bezel, but often a special claw setting will have to be devised, and this is always the case with roughs.

Not only are unfaceted stones technically more easy to set, but they offer much readier scope for originality and imagination in design. Above all they lend them-selves to complete integration into the piece, whereas the setting for a faceted stone almost always tends to emphasise the stone and thus to set it apart from its carrier.

## BEZEL SETTING

This setting is essentially a narrow metal band which fits closely round the base of the stone; its top edge is pressed inward over the inward curve of the stone and thus grips it.

Begin by determining the width of the bezel. It should be narrow in order to allow as much as possible of the stone to show, yet not so narrow that there is insufficient 'turn-in' to grip properly.

The thickness of metal used should be 4–6 B.M.G., depending on the size of the stone. In the case of silver it is best to use fine silver, which, being softer than sterling, can be turned in more easily.

Cut a strip of the right length. The circumference of the stone can be determined by placing the stone on the table, winding a piece of binding wire round its base and twisting the ends two or three times with a pair of pliers to produce a tight-fitting loop. Remove the loop, cut it and open out the ends. The length will give the length of the strip. If this method is not possible, perhaps because the stone is irregular in shape, or so small or steep sided that the wire just slips off, cut a strip that is obviously too long, fit it closely round the stone, mark the point of overlap and cut off the excess.

File the ends of the strip square, fit together by bending and solder with hard solder. The shape of the ring does not matter at this stage: a flat ring is in fact best since with this it is easier to get the ends to meet perfectly in line. The solder paillon should be placed on the outside of the joint and drawn through by applying heat on the inside. With the solder on the outside it is easy to clean away any excess afterwards. Pickle and wash.

The bezel must now be shaped to fit the stone, and this is done simply by placing the bezel on a flat surface and pressing the stone into it (41). The fit should be a sliding fit, not so tight that the stone has to be forced, not so loose that it can move. If the bezel is too small, stretch it by inserting a smooth steel rod and rolling it to and fro

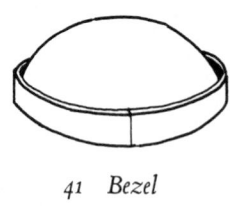

41  Bezel

42 *Bezel with bearer*

on a steel flat; test frequently while doing this, for it is easy to overstretch. If the bezel is too large, a piece will have to be cut out which should include at least the original joint, and the ends can then be re-soldered.

Check that the width of the bezel is even all round. First, to ensure that the base is absolutely flat, lay the bezel on a piece of fine emery paper on a flat surface and rub lightly until the surface is an even matt all over. Set the dividers to the narrowest width and scribe a line right round the top. File down to the line, then re-check for fit.

If the stone is to go on a flat piece of jewelry, the bezel can now be soldered on, using easy solder. Failing this, a backing of some kind will have to be provided. If the stone is opaque, with a flat base, this can be of sheet, 6 B.M.G. It is best fitted inside the bezel, and allowance for its thickness will have had to be made when determining the width of the bezel. Place the bezel on a piece of sheet and run the scriber round along the inside so as to get the exact shape. Cut out, fit and solder.

In the case of transparent or translucent stones, other considerations come into the picture. Normally such stones look brighter and better the more light is allowed to pass through them, and in such cases an open backing in the form of a bearer is called for. This has the additional advantage of allowing access for cleaning the back of the stone. Sometimes, however, the appearance of the stone can be improved by setting it on some coloured reflecting material—foiling the stone, and in such cases we shall still need a close backing.

A bearer is simply a wire, round, square or rectangular, fitted round the inside of the bezel and soldered, upon which the stone can rest. Care must, of course, be taken that it is absolutely level and set at the right height. If the base of the bearer is to be level with the base of the bezel no problem arises. If they are not to be level, then a line marking the top of the bearer will have to be scribed inside the bezel with dividers set to the depth the stone will occupy. Again its width should have been allowed for when determining the width of the bezel.

Such a bearer is needed also if the stone is to be mounted on a ring, and allowance has to be made for the curve of the shank. In this case the bezel has to be extra deep to allow for the curve which will have to be filed out in order to enable it to sit on the shank (*42*).

Again, a bearer is necessary if the base of the stone is not flat, as in a double cabochon or, often, a tumbled stone.

The stone is usually not mounted until the whole piece is complete and polished: this avoids any risk of damaging it during the polishing process.

In the case of a close-backed setting, one or two layers of paper should first be put in on which the stone can rest. The purpose is to take up any unevenness in the base which might cause the stone to rock and so loosen the bezel. If the stone is translucent or trans- parent this paper is often some foil, silver or coloured, to improve brightness or colour.

Foiling is a perfectly legitimate dodge, even though it can be—and has been—used for fraudulent purposes. There is nothing wrong in making a stone, or even a piece of glass, look its best: this, after all, is the whole purpose of a setting. What is wrong is then to misrepresent its character, to put forward a piece of glass, for instance, as a genuine amethyst. The choice of foil is a matter of trial and error, and trial and error can produce surprising results. Who would imagine, for instance, that a rather dull watery white opal showing only pale suggestions of blue would flash into life when placed on a black surface—but it happens.

The stone is set by being placed into the bezel which is then pressed inward into close contact all round. With a round or oval stone this can usually be done by rubbing along the edge with a burnisher, used with quite a firm pressure. At the start the burnisher should be applied at opposite points on the bezel in order to keep the stone centred. When the stone is firmly gripped at half a dozen points or so, the burnisher can then be drawn in smooth strokes along the whole edge until this lies smooth and even.

A burnisher is a piece of steel with a surface polished to a mirror finish and set in a handle. The normal shape for a jeweller is oval in section tapering to a point, about 3 inches long and with the pointed end bent in a gentle curve. This gives flat, concave and convex surfaces to use as may be best suited to the work. The surface polish must be maintained to perfection. This means protecting from rust and polishing from time to time on very fine emery paper, with a metal polish rub to finish. Burnishers made of agate can be obtained; they keep their surface, but are more expensive and nowadays rather hard to find.

If the bezel is too thick or too hard to respond satisfactorily to the burnisher, then a pusher will be needed. This is home-made, of $\frac{1}{8}$ inch square steel or brass about 1 inch long set in a handle so as to leave about $\frac{1}{2}$ inch projecting (43). Brass being soft leaves fewer marks on the bezel, but slips more easily: steel marks, but does not slip quite so easily. The tip should be bevelled off slightly all round. The end, too, should be filed to a slight bevel and have a few lines scored across the face to reduce the chances of slip.

In use the pusher is set against the edge of the bezel with its top slightly overlapping and pressed inwards: simultaneously the handle is raised until at the end the pusher is pressing almost vertically down on the edge of the bezel. This ensures a very close fit indeed. The process is repeated all along the bezel.

When the stone is firmly set, file the bezel all round to a neat

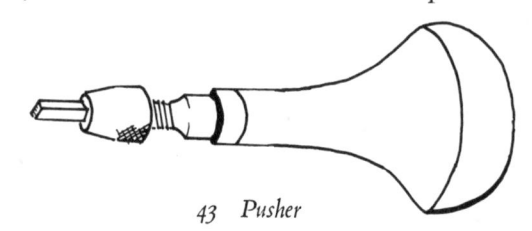

43   *Pusher*

feather edge, using a needle-file (and not forgetting that some stones, such as opals, are soft and may be damaged by the file). This will at the same time remove all marks left by the pusher. Polish by rubbing with the burnisher.

Square settings are dealt with in exactly the same way save for the corners, which should have a tiny V-shaped notch sawn out to enable the sides to meet neatly when they are turned in.

## SETTING FROM THE BACK

Sometimes a visible bezel may be out of place in the design. If the surface in which the stone is to be set is of fairly thick metal, equivalent to the bezel which this particular stone would require, cut and file a hole with sloping sides shaped to the stone as exactly as possible. Make and solder a narrow bezel on the underside. Fit the stone from the back so that its base does not sink in flush but projects about $\frac{1}{64}$ inch, and burnish the bezel over its edge (44). If the upper opening does not fit quite closely round the stone, press into contact with the burnisher or pusher and level the surface by stoning. Polish.

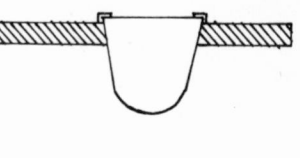
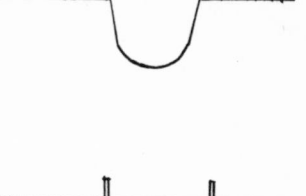

44 Setting from the back

## GIPSY SETTING

This is a setting giving a similar effect frequently employed for signet rings. It is applied only to flat-topped square and rectangular stones. The stone is set from the top into the thickness of the metal, and must therefore rest on a bearer which can be soldered in. A groove about $\frac{1}{32}$ inch deep is carved all round the edge of the opening and about $\frac{1}{32}$ inch away so as to leave a ridge which is in effect a bezel (45). The proper tool for this is a round-bottomed scorper (see p. 104). The stone is dropped in and the edge of the opening is closed by setting a flat punch against it and tapping lightly with a hammer. This must be done with great care since there is risk of damage to the stone. It is wise to use this setting only for the harder stones, such as agates.

When the stone is set the groove is cleaned up with the scorper. Alternatively if the stone is set deep enough, the whole surface can be filed and stoned. Finally polish.

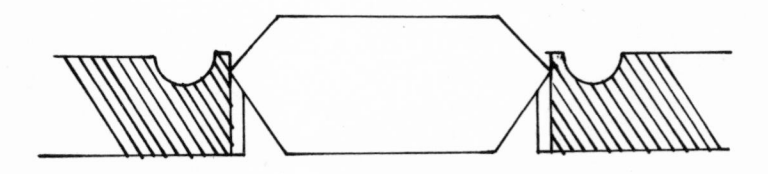

45 Gypsy setting

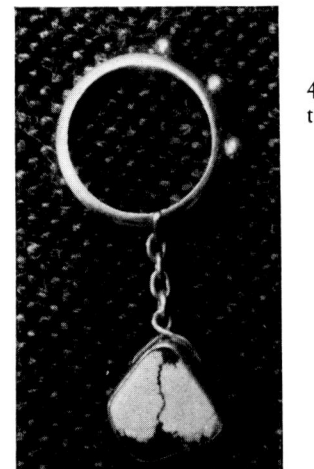

46 Ring, silver with three silver beads, turquoise matrix

47 Brooch, white quartz crystal, diamonds of gold, polished and textured by John Donald

48 Brooch, wulfenite and gold, by John Donald

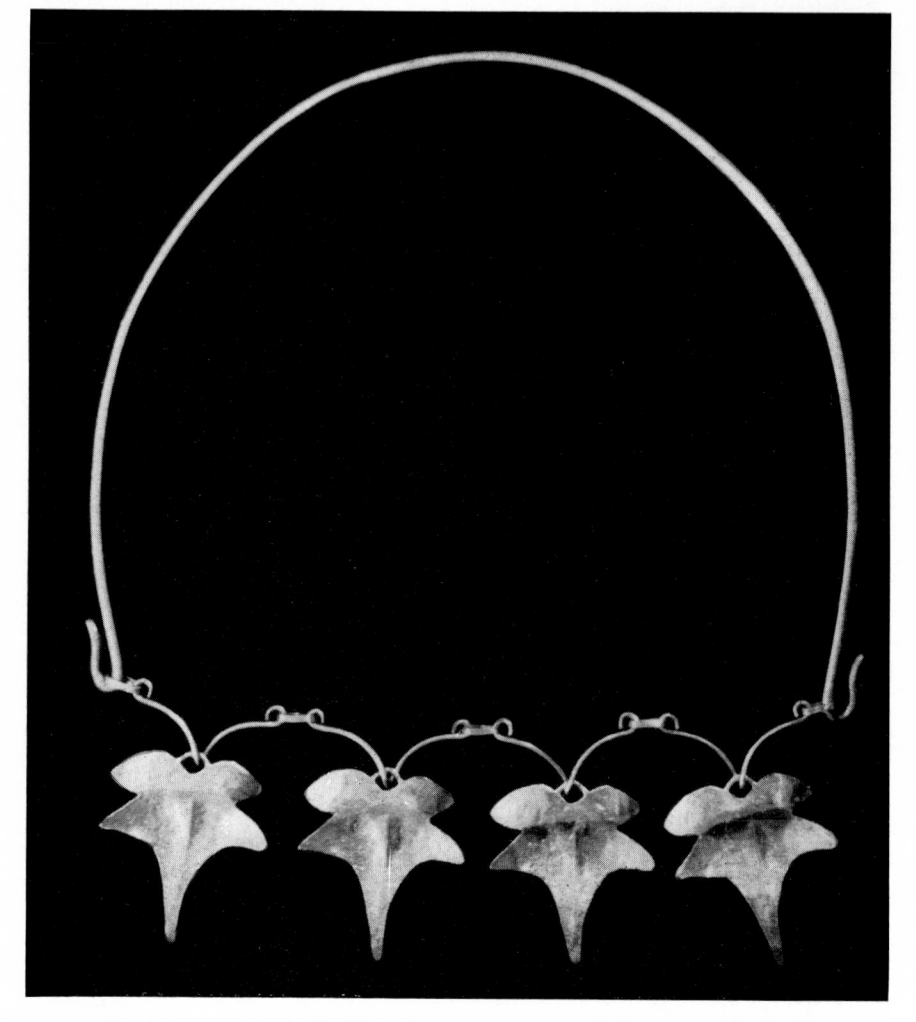

49  Necklace, silver repoussé and chased

# CLAW SETTING

Claw settings are used for faceted stones and are designed to allow the maximum light to reach the stone from all sides, thus giving it greater brilliance. Such settings also emphasise the stone by separating it from the piece which carries it. We shall describe two types, the coronet and the box, which are both rather formal, and which are both usually mounted by means of suitable shoulder-pieces. But there is no need to be tied to the conventional settings: it is always possible to design one's own—one such is illustrated (27)—and the problems to be solved always provide an interesting exercise.

## CORONET SETTING

For a round stone the first step is to make a conical collet. Take some sheet, about 10 B.M.G. or a little thicker, scribe a straight line equal in length to the diameter of the stone (50, 1 (a)). From its centre drop a perpendicular. Scribe another line (b) parallel with the first such that the perpendicular crosses it at its centre; its length is equal to whatever you may decide should be the small diameter of the cone, and its distance from the first line is not less than the distance from girdle to culet (point) of the stone. Join up the parallel lines by a line (c) which passes through their ends and cuts the perpendicular at (x); this gives you the centre for two arcs whose radii are the lengths (ca) and (cb). With the dividers step off on arc (a) a length three times that of the diameter of the girdle of the stone and join the end to the point (x). Cut out the shaded portion in the drawing (50, 2). The strip thus obtained is rounded to a cone, the ends are joined with hard solder, and the collet trued up on the triblet (50, 3).

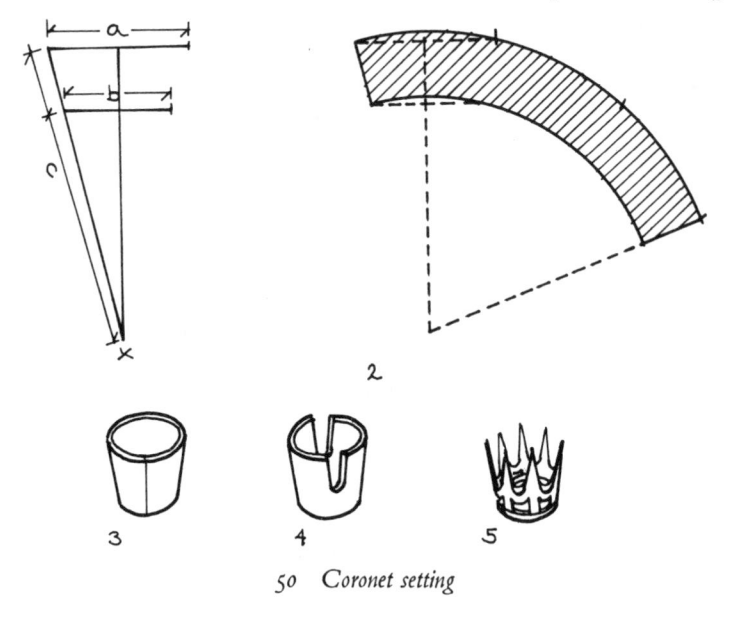

*50   Coronet setting*

On the top of the collet, mark out the position of the claws by drawing the saw straight across the centre. For an eight-claw setting repeat at right angles and again half-way between the marks. If the collet is small, it is best mounted with sealing wax on a short dowel rod, which enables it to be held firmly.

Now make eight vertical cuts half-way between the marks and approximately half-way down the collet, but avoid cutting the soldered joint (50, 4). Saw and file out the spaces so as to leave eight claws standing. Bevel off the bases between and also, if you wish, the sides of the claws, but be careful not to weaken them unduly by removing too much metal.

Reverse the collet and saw and file some decorative motif all round the base (50, 5). Finish by soldering on one or two rings, then polish and mount.

To set the stone, place it on the collet and bend the claws either in or out until the girdle rests on about half their thickness evenly all round. Remove the stone and with a scorper carve out this half-thickness leaving a ledge on the inside for the stone to rest on at such a depth as will leave sufficient claw projecting above the girdle to turn in and grip. With pliers turn in any two adjacent claws, insert the stone and close the opposite two claws by burnishing them over. Repeat with the remaining claws, and when the stone is firmly set with no trace of rocking, tidy up the ends of the claws with file and burnisher.

The same process can be adopted for square and rectangular stones. A round collet is made as before, but after it has been soldered its sides instead of being trued up on a triblet, are carefully flattened with flat pliers to give the rectangular shape. Top and bottom are then filed level and claws marked out at the corners and, if desired, in the sides.

The disadvantage of this method is that the corners of the setting are rounded to some extent, but if the metal is thick enough they can be sharpened with a file.

## BOX FRAME SETTING (51)

This is a simple modern setting for round, square, or rectangular settings, but it requires a certain amount of dexterity in securing the components together when soldering.

Using square wire, 10 or 12 B.M.G. thick, make up two round rings or two rectangular rings. The round rings are, of course, for round stones and their sizes must be such that the outside diameter of the larger ring is that of the girdle of the stone so that this can rest upon it; the diameter of the smaller ring is that of the base of the setting. The two rings are in effect the top and the base of the collet described for the coronet setting. Similarly the larger of the rectangular rings will be the same size (outside) as the girdle of the rectangular stone.

Using 10 B.M.G. sheet, cut four wedge-shaped strips about $\frac{3}{32}$ inch wide tapering to about $\frac{1}{32}$ inch and a little longer than the height of the setting with claws. Bend the excess length to almost a right angle. File a slight bevel on the edges of the rings where the claws are to go (the corners in the case of the rectangular rings). Now

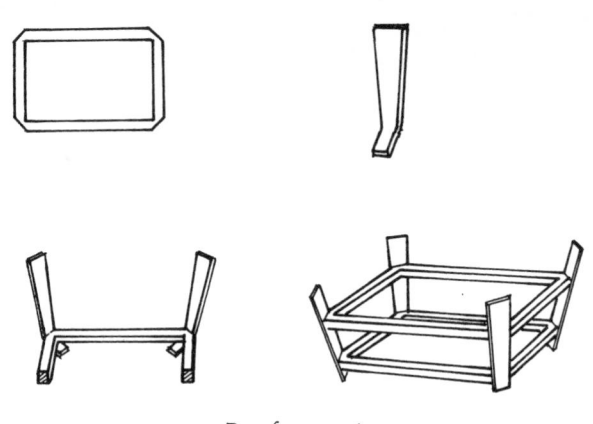

51   *Box frame setting*

arrange the strips round the smaller ring standing it on the turned⁄over portions and so keeping the strips upright but slightly splayed out, and solder. Make sure that the soldering is sound on the sides. An alternative method is to support the ring at a height and hook the strips to it, clipping them to ensure that they splay out slightly.

This arrangement forms the base of the box. The upper ring, again suitably bevelled, is placed inside the uprights at the correct height, leaving about $\frac{1}{8}$ inch projecting above. It will be gripped in position by the uprights, but make sure that it is properly centred between them and parallel with the lower ring. Wire if necessary and solder.

To complete, file off the turned⁄over portions on the base, leaving it flat, and polish. Place the stone in the top resting on the top ring, and bend the claws over, then file and burnish them.

If you prefer the box to have straight instead of tapered sides, the two rings must be made the same size.

# CHAPTER VI

## *Gemstones*

When the amateur jeweller chooses stones for his jewelry, he may be led by a variety of motives: he may be attracted by certain colours, or by the desire to find a stone not too delicate for experimental handling, he may want a very large one, an unusually shaped one, a not too expensive one, etc. Some guidance is useful, though here it can only be fairly summary: the body of available knowledge is very large.

It is, of course, best to buy stones from a reputable dealer who will give exact information about what you buy and quote a correct price. People can be lucky enough to pick up bargains in street markets, and as far as the inexpensive agates and polished pebbles go, there is no great risk involved. But in the higher price-range there are too many synthetic or dyed stones pretending to be the real thing at an inflated price.

If we take the question of price first: the most expensive are of the group known as precious stones. To this group belong diamonds, emeralds, rubies and sapphires. All other stones are known as semi-precious, and this group includes hundreds of types. The division is a traditional one, not very meaningful when the value of a particular stone comes to be considered. Particular semi-precious stones, good opals and pearls, for instance, can be more valuable than precious stones; and much rarer, too—alexandrites, for instance, in comparison with which all the precious stones are common.

Most stones are natural minerals (though some may be dyed or heat-treated to change their colour). In addition there are nowadays synthetic stones made to imitate certain natural minerals such as rubies and sapphires. Chemically they are of the same

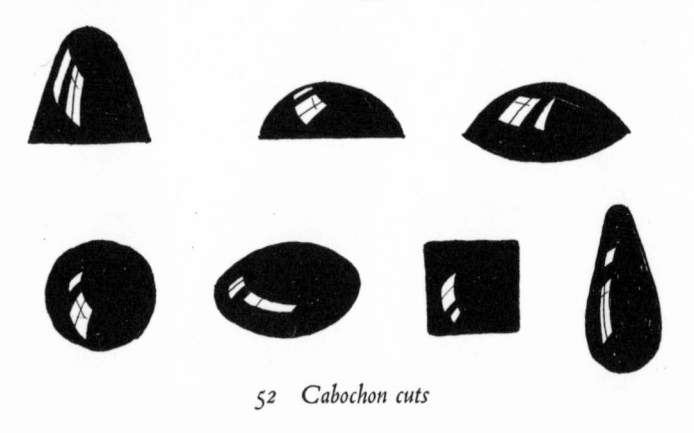

52   *Cabochon cuts*

constitution and structure as the stone they imitate, and their colour is first class. They are cheap, and in most cases distinguishable from the genuine article by their very perfection.

From the animal or vegetable kingdoms come amber, jet, pearl and coral, and all of these except real pearls can be bought at quite low cost. Real pearls are round pearls produced by the oyster without any assistance from man. Cultured pearls are just as real, but the oyster is induced to produce them by the insertion of a small foreign body in its mantle. Misshapen natural pearls are known as blister pearls and baroque pearls, according to type; and in addition there are pearls of inferior colour produced by fresh-water oysters.

Lastly, there are imitation stones known as *pastes*, and usually made of coloured glass. There is prejudice against them, but they have an honorable history. Our museums contain many most beautiful antique jewels which mount nothing but paste.

Many of the mineral stones occur naturally in the form of crystals of varying shape and structure, singly or in clusters, large and small. Such crystals have been used most successfully by present-day jewelry designers, and in such exclusive company as the 1964 Diamonds International Award Exhibition not only did numerous entries feature natural crystals, such as amethyst, topaz and rose quartz, but three of the twenty-six top awards displayed them. Another winning design was created from snowflake obsidian and diamond, which demonstrates that today pattern and texture are trendsetters, and materials are not chosen for their intrinsic value alone.

Stones not suitable for use in their natural state must be cut and polished, or tumbled. In Chapter V we have already mentioned the forms in which cut stones appear. We illustrate the usual cabochon cuts(52) and also examples of faceted stones(53).

The important characteristics of gemstones are hardness, colour and certain other features possessed by some, but not all stones.

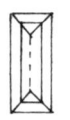 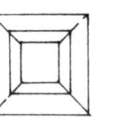 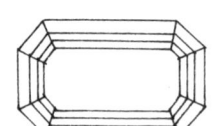

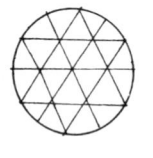 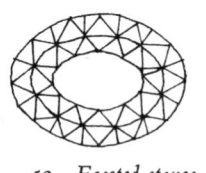 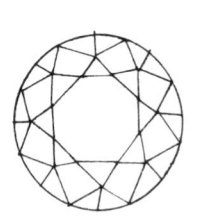

53   Faceted stones

The significance of hardness is that it represents durability in wear. Among gemmologists, therefore, hardness is defined as the ability to scratch other stones when rubbed against them, or conversely, to resist being scratched. In 1822 an Austrian scientist, Friedrich Mohs, worked out a scale which has become universally accepted under the name 'Mohs' Scale'. It is in fact not so much a scale as a list of gradings, from 1–10, with no real relationship between the grades. Diamond is at the top of the scale with 10; ruby and sapphire are both rated as 9, but the difference in hardness between 10 and 9 in Mohs' Scale is much greater than the difference between 9 and 1. Nevertheless the scale is useful. Thus it is true to say that gemstones having a hardness of less than 6 will not wear well when mounted on finger rings or bracelets, though they will do better on necklaces where they are much more protected.

So far as colour is concerned, nature knows no limit. Every conceivable colour and shade will be found. The table given on pp. 72–4 lists a number of the commoner stones under colours, and shows also the hardness on Mohs' Scale. The colours given are only approximations: a blue sapphire, for instance, may be anything from a pale blue-grey to a deep inky-blue verging on the black. Differences of this kind are likely to be reflected in the price. Thus, the best turquoises are nowadays considered to be the robin's-egg-blue ones, and they will be more expensive than pale blue turquoises or those showing a greenish-blue.

As already mentioned, apart from hardness and colour certain stones possess individual characteristics which form part of their appeal.

*Schiller* is a kind of luminescence like a pool of moonlight trapped in the depth of the stone. It is to this that the moonstone owes its name. Schiller should be bluish in colour, but is often merely white and the stone is then correspondingly less valued. The precious opal shows a *play of colour*, a flashing iridescence caused by the fact that the stone is made up of layers of silica with microscopic pockets of water between which break up and refract the light. Opals which do not have this play of colour, and are not rated as 'precious opals', display however, *opalescence*, a softly gleaming white which moonstones also possess.

*Asterism* is a characteristic which may be found in several kinds of stone, principally rubies and sapphires. Stones in which this occurs are translucent rather than trans-parent, and they happen to have inclusions of a different mineral orientated in a particular way. A stone of this kind must be cut *en cabochon*, and the cut properly orientated in relation to the inclusions. If then one looks into it one will see a four- or a six-pointed star, more or less strongly defined according to the quality of the stone. 'Star' stones tend to be fascinating rather than beautiful, for their colour is usually not outstanding. Star sapphires in particular, which are by no means uncommon, are usually a cloudy grey-blue very different from the rich delphinium blue of a good quality ordinary sapphire.

*Chatoyancy* is a streak of light one finds in some stones, like a shining band, caused by various inclusions such as asbestos fibres, for instance. Such stones must be cut *en cabochon*. The light strikes the inclusions and they light up like cats' eyes in the dark.

70

Cat's eye, Tiger's eye and Labradorite, all quartz stones, display this quality. A much more valuable chatoyant stone is the oriental cat's eye or chrysoberyl, not a quartz, but of the beryl family. Chrysoberyl also occurs in another form, the alexandrite, a very rare and valuable stone with *dichroic* character or two-colour appearance: in this case dark green in daylight, deep violet-red by artificial light.

Tourmalines have a characteristic known as *zoning*, that is two or more colours may occur in the same crystal with a sharp line of demarcation in between. The most common variety has rather the appearance of a stripy sweet, bright pink inside surrounded by an outer layer of green.

Reading books about stones is of great help when buying stones as one learns what qualities to look for. Apart from the usefulness of this information, imagination cannot remain unmoved by the tradition, romance and superstition attached to the histories of the great gemstones of the world. The legendary name of Golconda was synonymous with inexhaustible richness, and the Koh-i-noor symbolised in its blaze of light the very peak of power. Tales of precious stones abound with glorious extravagance. One of the richest pictures is conjured up by Sir Harry Luke, describing in an article in *The Times* a visit to a vault housing the treasures of the Iranian State. The article was appropriately called 'Aladdin's Caves full of Jewels' and the visitor duly stubbed his toe against mounds, a foot high, of diamonds, emeralds, rubies and sapphires. But the Golden Globe is the trophy one would like to have carried off: 'The first object the visitor then encountered was a large revolving golden globe on a solid gold stand, the continents shown in compact masses of rubies, the oceans in emeralds, the Equator and the Tropics outlined in diamonds. By means of this decorative apparatus were the little Qajar princes taught their geography.'

# A List of Stones

| TRANSPARENT STONES | MOHS' SCALE |
|---|---|
| *Blue* | |
| Aquamarine | 7½ |
| Sapphire | 9 |
| Spinel | 8 |
| Zircon | 7½ |
| *Green* | |
| Alexandrite (by day) | 8½ |
| Demantoid | 6½–7½ |
| Emerald | 8 |
| Spinel | 8 |
| Tourmaline | 7–7½ |
| Peridot | 6½–7 |
| Sapphire | 9 |
| *Red* | |
| Alexandrite (by artificial light) | 8½ |
| Almandite | 7½ |
| Garnet | 6½–7½ |
| Ruby | 9 |
| Spinel | 8 |
| Zircon | 7½ |
| *Purple* | |
| Amethyst | 7 |
| *Pink* | |
| Morganite (pink beryl) | 7½ |
| Ruby | 9 |
| Topaz (true) | 8–9 |
| Tourmaline | 7–7½ |
| *Yellow* | |
| Beryl | 7½ |
| Citrine | 7 |
| Sapphire | 9 |
| Topaz (true) | 8–9 |
| Topaz (quartz) | 7 |
| Zircon | 7½ |
| *Brown* | |
| Smoky Quartz (also known as Cairngorm) | 7 |

| TRANSPARENT STONES | MOHS' SCALE |
|---|---|
| *Clear* | |
| Diamond | 10 |
| Quartz (rock crystal) | 7 |
| Spinel | 8 |
| Zircon | $7\frac{1}{2}$ |

TRANSLUCENT STONES

*Blue*

| Sapphire (star) | 9 |
|---|---|

*Green*

| Agate (moss) | 7 |
|---|---|
| Chrysoprase | 7 |
| Jade | $6\frac{1}{2}$–7 |

*Red*

| Agate | 7 |
|---|---|
| Carnelian | 7 |
| Ruby (star) | 9 |

*Pink*

| Jade | $6\frac{1}{2}$–7 |
|---|---|
| Rose Quartz | 7 |

*Yellow*

| Agate | 7 |
|---|---|
| Chrysoberyl (cat's eye) | $8\frac{1}{2}$ |
| Amber | $2$–$2\frac{1}{2}$ |

*Brown*

| Agate | 7 |
|---|---|
| Amber | $2$–$2\frac{1}{2}$ |

*Black*

| Agate | 7 |
|---|---|
| Obsidian | 7 |
| Onyx | 7 |

*White*

| Agate | 7 |
|---|---|
| Chalcedony | 7 |
| Moonstone | 6 |
| Opal (and all colours) | 6 |

*Blue*

| | |
|---|---|
| Lapis Lazuli | 6 |
| Labradorite | 6–7 |
| Pearl | 3½ |
| Turquoise | 6 |

*Green*

| | |
|---|---|
| Agate | 7 |
| Aventurine | 6 |
| Bloodstone (red speckled) | 7 |
| Jade | 6½–7 |
| Labradorite | 6–7 |
| Malachite | 4–5 |
| Turquoise | 6 |

*Red*

| | |
|---|---|
| Agate | 7 |
| Coral | 3½ |
| Jasper | 7 |

*Pink*

| | |
|---|---|
| Coral | 3½ |
| Jade | 6½–7 |
| Pearl | 3½ |

*Yellow*

| | |
|---|---|
| Agate | 7 |
| Amber | 2–2½ |
| Labradorite | 6–7 |

*Brown*

| | |
|---|---|
| Agate | 7 |
| Tiger's Eye | 7 |

*Black*

| | |
|---|---|
| Agate | 7 |
| Haematite | 6½ |
| Jet | 3½ |
| Obsidian | 5 |
| Onyx | 7 |

# CHAPTER VII

## *Finger Rings*

The basis of a ring is the shank, and to make this truly round a former of some kind will be needed. A short length of round steel rod, polished, will do, but a more efficient tool is the ring mandrel or triblet, a length of round steel rod 10–14 inches long including the handle, and tapered so that its varying diameter covers the whole range of finger ring sizes. In choosing such a mandrel, give preference to the longer one, which has a more gradual taper. Some mandrels are made grooved and marked to indicate the standard ring sizes (8). If this is not obtainable, you will need a sizing-stick which does have those markings, but is made of plastic or brass and is therefore not sufficiently strong to enable a ring to be formed on it.

It is useful also to have a set of standard rings which can be slipped on to the finger to determine its size.

The shank can be made of wire, round, half-round, oval, rectangular, square or any fancy section, or of strip cut from sheet. Thickness and width are a matter of taste, depending upon whether the design of the ring is light and delicate, or heavy. Commercial rings are commonly 13 or 14 B.M.G. for a woman's ring, and 18 or 19 B.M.G. for a man's ring.

Having settled the width and section of the material, the first step is to determine the length required. A simple, though not very accurate method is to measure off on a band of paper passed round the *knuckle* of the ring finger and add twice the thickness of the metal to the length thus obtained. A better alternative is to try out the standard rings until the right size has been found, measure the internal diameter (or look this up in Appendix 2), add twice the thickness of the metal and multiply by three.

It is wise to make the ring a little smaller than the indicated size, say half a size smaller, since the final polishing will remove sufficient material to bring the ring up to the proper size. On the other hand, if the shank is to be very wide, it should be on the large side, for if it is tight-fitting it will be not only uncomfortable to wear, but also very difficult to take off.

Cut a strip to length, file the ends square, bend over to meet, and solder with hard solder. Do not worry about the shape at this stage, for the ring will be trued up later. Do not worry either about wiring it: if the ends are bent to overlap, then sprung together, they will remain in position when the heat is applied. The solder should be placed on the outside, and the flame used to draw it through to the inside.

When the joint is made, pickle and file off any excess solder.

The next step is to true up the ring. If your mandrel is a length of rod fix it

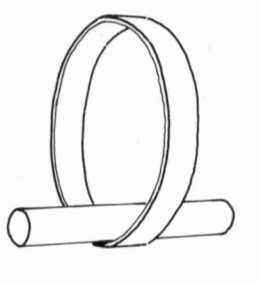

54    *Trueing a ring*

horizontally in the vice, leaving one end projecting, slip the ring on to this and hammer with the rawhide mallet, turning the ring all the while until it is true or almost so. When satisfied as to this, take the rod out of the vice, slip the ring on again, and roll to and fro on a hard surface, preferably a steel plate (*54*).

With a ring mandrel the process is very nearly the same, but because the mandrel is tapered, the ring will have to be turned round from time to time during the initial hammering so that it does not become cone-shaped. The final rolling is omitted. Instead the ring is driven towards the thicker part of the mandrel with very gentle taps on the edge; it must be pulled back just sufficiently to free it after each blow, and kept turning. The ring is then reversed and the process repeated from the other side.

When the ring has been trued up it can be tried for size. With a marked mandrel, this will, of course, show automatically; otherwise try it on the sizing-stick or on the finger, if available.

If the ring is too small, it can be stretched by gentle hammering on the rod or mandrel; use a flat-faced hammer and turn the ring all the while so that no two consecutive blows fall in the same place. Stretching is fairly rapid, so check the size frequently. If the ring is too large, a section, which must include the joint, will have to be cut out, the joint re-made, and the ring trued up again.

So much for the shank which, with no further treatment than final polishing, would in fact be an ordinary plain ring.

If, however, it is to carry a stone, then this is a matter which must be taken into account in the design. The essential principle, of course, is simple: it is that the stone should be held securely. This means that the materials must be sufficiently substantial, and there must be sufficient soldered area, having regard to the size, weight and shape of the stone. Normally the question is whether or not to use shoulder pieces. When this has been decided, the question is how to design the work so that it has individuality and character, and enhances the appearance of the stone. The problems posed are few, the possible solutions numerous. Take for instance the mounting of a simple round cabochon set in a closed bezel. Here are three possible solutions:

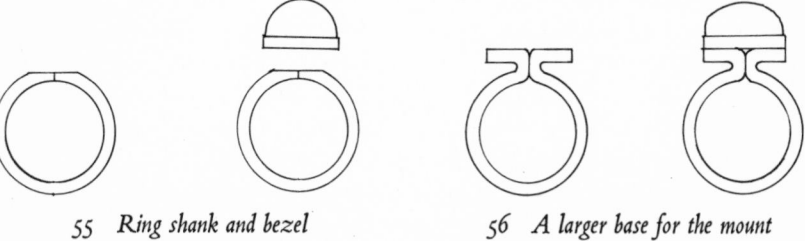

55    *Ring shank and bezel*                    56    *A larger base for the mount*

The simplest is to file a flat on the side of the ring (above the joint) and solder the base of the bezel on to this (55). Such a solution would be satisfactory if the mount is not too large, and the shank reasonably wide or thick: in other words, dimensions must be such that the soldered area is sufficiently large in relation to the size of the mount to provide an adequately strong base of attachment.

An alternative solution, providing a larger base for the mount, is shown (56). Here the strip for the shank is cut sufficiently long to enable the ends to be bent back to form a table. They are soldered together on the bend, and this is filed flat to provide an adequate soldering surface. Trueing a shank of this kind would seem more difficult than trueing a plain shank, since one cannot hammer evenly all round, but the difficulty is more apparent than real: tapping the edges of the shank on the mandrel will achieve the desired result.

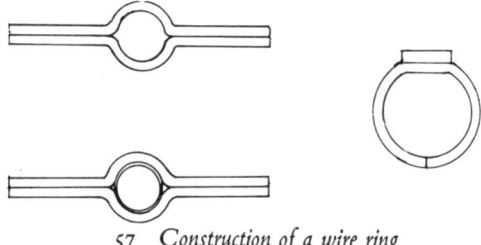

57   *Construction of a wire ring*

The third solution is based on the use of round wire, and is shown in the photograph (63) and drawing (57). Two lengths of wire are cut (on the generous side because it is not possible to calculate the necessary length) and their centres bent round the bezel. The straight ends are wired together and soldered, using as little solder as possible in order to avoid flooding the joint which should appear clean and crisp. Next shape and size the shank, cut off any excess length of wire, solder and true up. This will close up the surround for the bezel a little: instead of opening it out again (which in any case would make the shank smaller) file a flat on the inside of the surround just sufficient so that the bezel can be slipped in and soldered. The advantage of this filing is that the flat will offer a larger soldering area than the round wire. In soldering the bezel into position, be careful that the portion which will have to be turned down to hold the stone is not soldered to the surround but projects above it, for otherwise the stone cannot be set. This is a setting problem which must always be borne in mind when designing a mount.

The leverage on a stone mount resulting from an accidental knock, even one so slight that the wearer does not notice it, can be very considerable, with corresponding risk to the security of the mount. Frequently, therefore, shoulders have to be provided to give additional support.

Once again various solutions are possible.

One of the simplest was devised for a square opaque stone and is shown in figure 58. An ordinary silver ring shank was made and another strip soldered round it to provide two projecting ends for supports. A great deal of solder (soft) is required to make sure that it floods through and makes the two surfaces adhere everywhere. The ring was shaped with the file. The outer surface of the shank and shoulders were worked with the file to create a textured finish; all other surfaces were

58   *Providing ends for supports*      59   *Attaching*      60   *Mount*
                                             *shoulders*         *with shoulders*

polished. For the ring illustrated a lapidary was asked to drill two holes in opposite sides of the stone. Corresponding holes were drilled into the shoulders, and the stone was fixed by wire pegs driven in and riveted and the heads filed smooth. It would have been equally simple—though the appearance would have been different —to have made a square bezel for the stone and soldered this into position between the shoulders, and either suspended above the shank or soldered to this as well.

More conventional are the shoulders illustrated in the drawing (59), which is almost self-explanatory. The shoulders are wedge-shaped and they are soldered (using clips to hold them in position) into notches filed in the side of the shank. Before being soldered, the base of the shoulders is thinned on the inside with a file in order to increase the soldering area and to ensure that the outside runs smoothly into the shank. Lastly a file is run straight across the top of the shoulders to ensure a level surface, and a flat is filed on the shank half-way between the shoulders. The bezel can be set between the shoulders, or these can be filed down level with the top of the shank so that the bezel rests on all three.

An alternative method is shown in the photograph (65) and the detail (60). Here two flat wires were soldered to the edge of the bezel on opposite sides to form the shoulders and then bent to the correct angle. The bezel being open, another flat wire was soldered straight across its base and the ends bent over to form claws similar to those formed by the shoulder pieces. The whole arrangement was soldered on to a flat filed on the ring shank, and the shoulders filed to meet the shank approximately at right angles.

Also illustrated is a ring mounting a raw amethyst crystal in which the shoulders are the mount (91). They were designed to be offset so that the stone should be held diagonally across the shank, and the problem was to solder

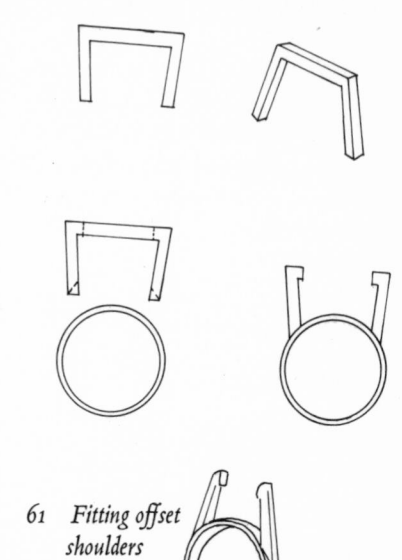

61   *Fitting offset shoulders*

78

them on so as to achieve the correct angle. The solution is shown (61). Square wire is bent into a bridge shape, with the legs set off at the required angle. The tips of the legs are filed off to fit the side of the shank. A wire through the shank and across the top of the bridge holds them together for soldering. The upper portion of the bridge is then sawn out and socket holes carved in the ends to receive the stone. The shoulders are filed to shape, the stone fitted between, and very gentle hammering drives them together sufficiently to grip. However, in order not to have to close the shoulders so tightly that the stone could not move, which would have risked damaging its tips, a touch of Araldite, which is an ideal adhesive for many purposes including the present one, was placed in the sockets, so that the stone was in fact glued in position.

# CHAPTER VIII

## *Wire Work*

Wire in jewelry is all-pervasive, its uses ranging from the modest adjunct of a brooch-pin and hinge through chain to applied decoration and constructions made up entirely of wire. And the word means rather more in jewelry than is normally understood in everyday language, where wire is just thin metal strip of round section. For decorative purposes wire can be round, half-round, oval, square, rectangular, triangular, knife-edged or even gadroon, ogee or star-shaped in section. Some of these types, round, half-round, square and rectangular, can be bought over the counter, in a wide range of gauges. But this is an extravagant way of doing things, resulting in a considerable stocking of materials which may be needed only rarely.

It is more useful, and certainly more economic, to lay in a couple of yards of round and square wire, say 14 S.W.G., and draw down to section and gauge as needed. This means investing in drawplates.

A drawplate (62) is a plate of hardened steel, about 5 inches long by $1\frac{1}{2}$ inches wide and $\frac{1}{4}$ inch thick, having a series of holes—20, 30 or 50, graduated in size and tapering from back to front. The holes may be round, square or any of the sections mentioned, and it is possible to obtain plates having three different shaped sections.

One plate with round holes and one with square holes, ranging in size from about 2 mm. down, will suffice for all normal purposes, and will enable one to produce not only round and square sections, but also half-round, quarter-round and oblong.

The drawing process is straightforward. Fix the plate in a vice equipped with clamps. Take a convenient length of wire, taper one end by filing down or hammering the last inch or so, find the smallest hole which will accept the wire, then insert the tapered end from the back of the plate into the next smaller one. Grip the projecting pointed end with a pair of pliers, and with a steady pull draw the wire straight

62  *Round drawplate and other available shapes*

63  Ring, silver gilt and moonstone

64  Ring, copper, silver-plated and blue enamels

65  Ring, silver and rutilated quartz

66  Two rings by Gerda Flockinger;
top,  silver  and  champlevé  enamel;
bottom, silver and tourmalines

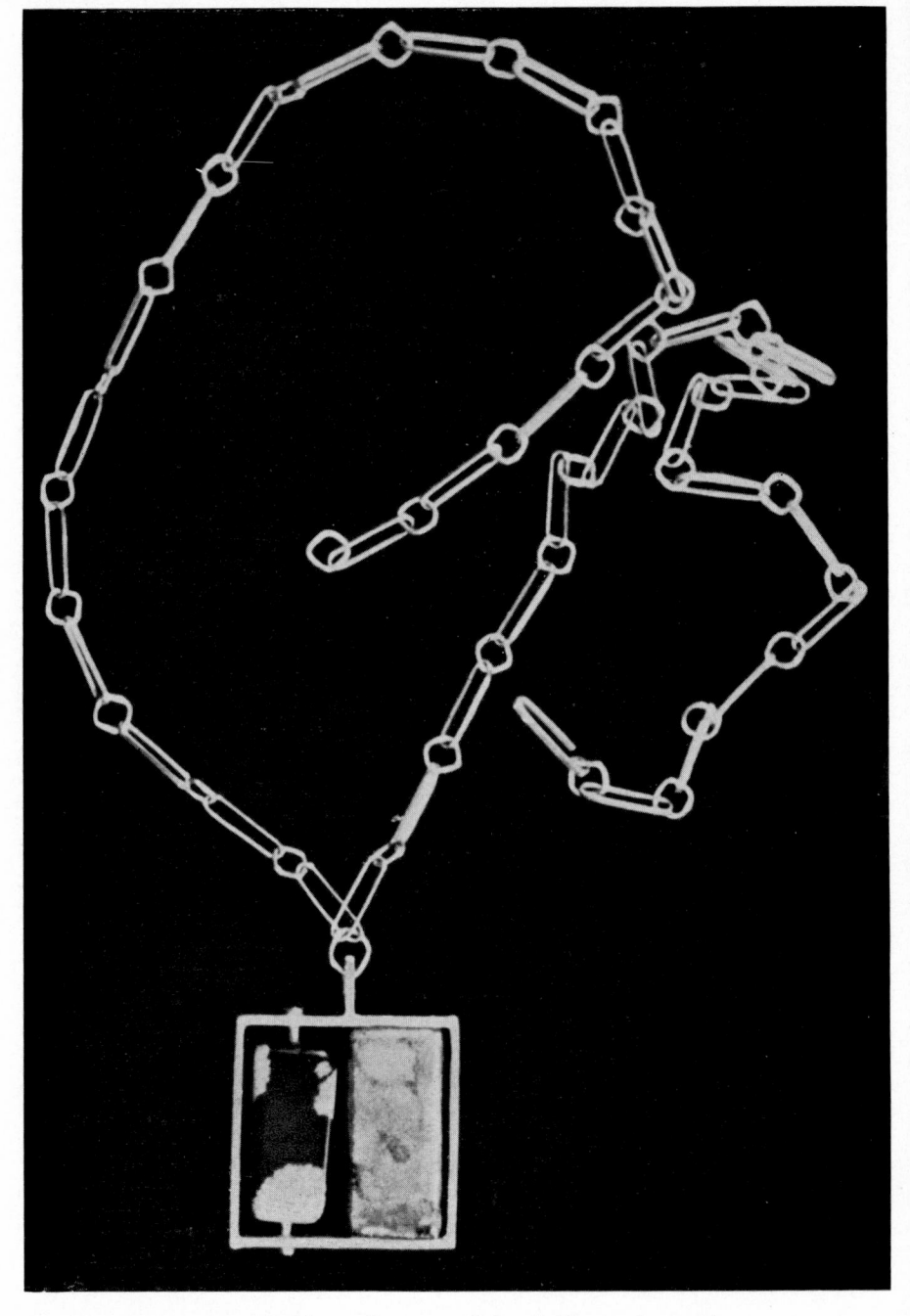

67  Necklace, silver, snowflake obsidian and enamel

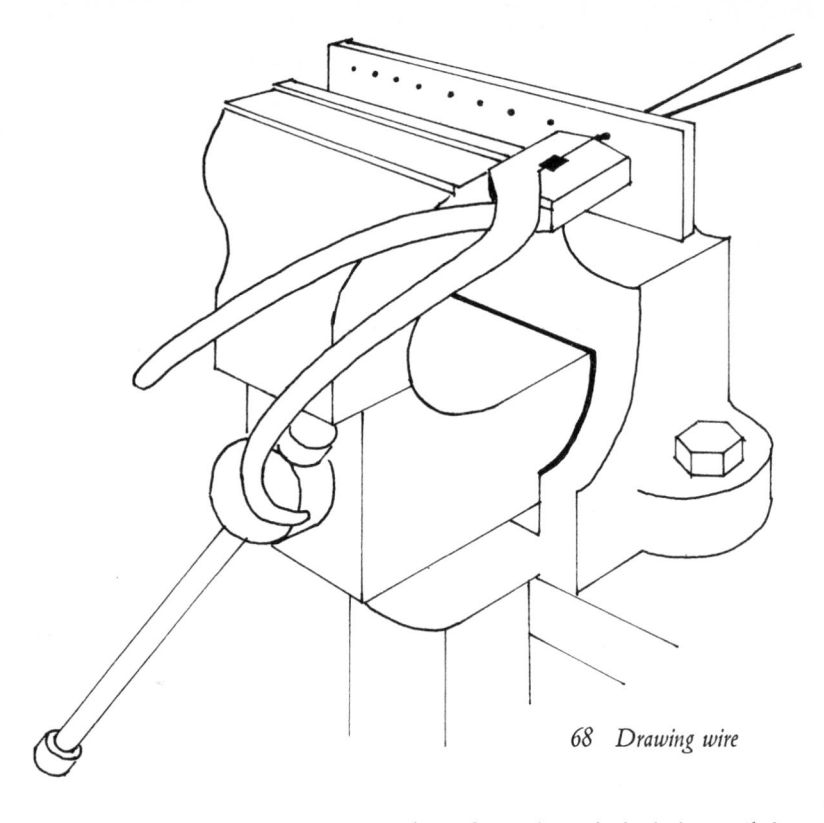

*68   Drawing wire*

through the hole (68). Repeat the process, working down through the holes until the wire has been reduced to the desired thickness.

A few points to remember:

Before drawing down, the wire should always be carefully annealed, for otherwise not only is the work unnecessarily hard, but the wire is liable to break. Annealing should be repeated every five or six holes, or even more often when working with a thick material which very quickly becomes hard and stiff. The most convenient way to handle a length of wire on the charcoal block is to form it into a small coil, winding one end of the wire two or three times round the coil to prevent it from straightening out as the heat is applied.

To make drawing more easy, grease the wire by pulling it across a block of beeswax, or apply a drop or two of machine oil to each hole in the plate.

Special draw tongs are available with the end of one handle bent back into a hook to give a better grip (68), but an ordinary, reasonably heavy pair of electrician's flat-nosed pliers, with well-serrated jaws, will serve quite adequately well.

The wire should be drawn through in one pull. If the pull is interrupted this will leave a small kink which may lead to a breakage the next time through. Both for this reason, and in the interest of economy, the wire should be no longer than is needed for the job in hand, and in any case no longer than can be managed in one pull, say about 2 feet. A sensible thing to do the first time a drawplate is used is to make a note of how much a given length of wire will stretch as it is drawn through each hole: this will later enable a reasonably exact calculation to be made of the amount of stockwire needed for any particular job.

We have mentioned the possibility of producing different shaped sections from the same drawplate. This involves pulling two or more wires through simultaneously. Thus a pair of square wires, of the same gauge, passed through the round holes will produce two half-round wires, or oblong wires if drawn through the square holes. Two half-round wires through the square holes will produce triangular sections if the flats are in line with the diagonals of the squares, or oblong wires if the flats are lined up parallel with the sides.

The methods described produce straightforward plain sections, but fancy sections too can be evolved, and there is plenty of scope here for experiment. Thus by way of illustration, two flat wires drawn through the round plate will produce wires flat on one side, but with the edges on the other side rounded and raised, leaving a groove between to form a kind of U-section.

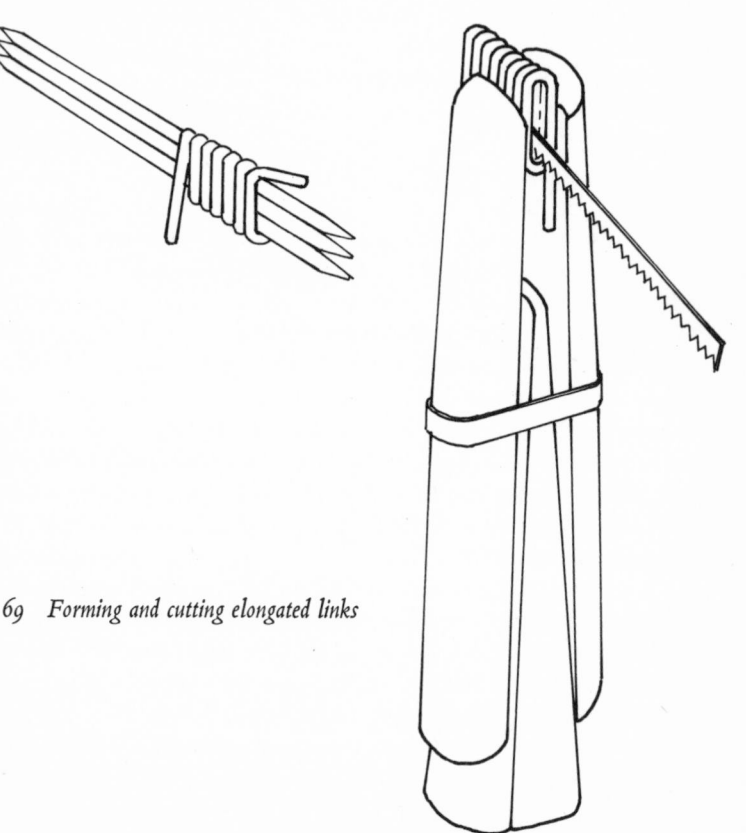

69   *Forming and cutting elongated links*

84

The most obvious use for wire is in chain-making. Here there are two problems, one the repetition work involved in making numerous links, and the other the question of soldering the ends of the links to ensure security.

In modern jewelry the need for repetition work can sometimes be burked, for it is possible to make up an attractive chain out of irregular-shaped links which are all different. Such treatment, however, tends to make the chain the dominant feature, and in many cases, therefore, will not be suitable.

To make numerous links of exactly the same shape we need a former or a kind of jig. For a simple round link this will be a length of rod. Steel is ideal. It can be the shank of a twist drill, or a knitting needle, or even a round nail. Wood, such as a length of dowelling or a pencil, will do as well. The only important consideration is that the former should be reasonably smooth and of the right diameter—allowing for the thickness of wire to be used—to produce the size of ring wanted.

The wire can be almost any section, round, oval, half-round, square, etc., and any thickness. It should be well annealed, then wound by hand as closely and evenly as possible round the former. Each turn will produce one link, but it is as well not to put on too many at a time, since they may be difficult to hold later when they come to be sawn: cover about one inch of the former, and repeat if necessary.

If the former is of wood, the rings can now be sawn through while still in position. If the former is metal, the coil should be slipped off and then sawn. In either case the cut should be as nearly as possible in line with the axis of the coil; where the coil has been removed from the former, this is more easily done if the sawblade is threaded through the coil and the sawing is done from the centre outwards (69).

Square, rectangular and oval links are made in similar fashion, but the former will obviously have to be square, rectangular, or oval, as the case may be. Copper or brass wire can be drawn to produce a square or rectangular section, built up to the right size, if necessary, by using two or more lengths side by side. Similarly, for oval rings two or more knitting needles side by side will serve, and an odd number of needles, with the centre one thicker than the outer ones, will produce a well-rounded oval.

Even well-annealed wire has a slight amount of spring left in it, or perhaps this develops as it is coiled, giving rise to a slight tendency to straighten out. In the case of round rings this is not noticeable, but other shaped rings will tend to bind on the former, making it sometimes difficult to remove the coil, and then, when it has been removed, tending to deform the coil and thus making it more difficult to cut.

In these cases, particularly square and rectangular links, it is best to use metal formers and to begin by winding on one or two layers of newspaper before making the coil. When the coil is made, anneal it on its former: this will ensure that it keeps its shape, and by burning the paper will leave a slight clearance, making it easy to pull off.

Oval and rectangular links should be cut at the ends, for the joints will then be hidden when the chain is made up.

After sawing, any roughnesses on the cut ends should be cleaned up with a file, and half the links can then be closed up and soldered. Closing or opening a link is

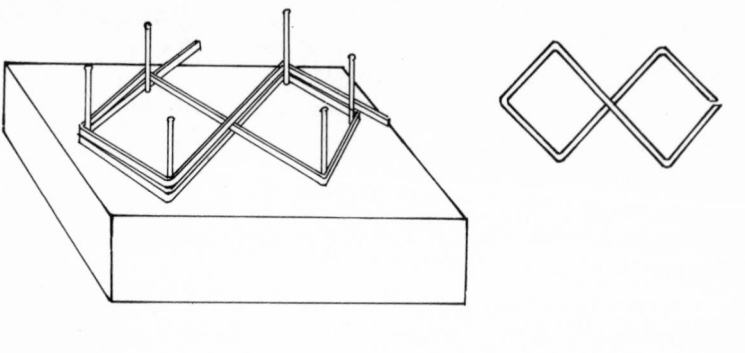

70　A jig for making double links

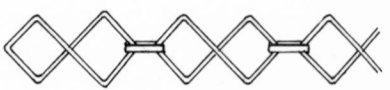

never done by pulling the ends outwards, but by twisting them sideways. This avoids distorting their shapes. To close, bend inwards to a slight overlap, then spring together, and the ends will remain closed when being soldered.

The chain can now be completed by joining an open link to two closed ones and soldering. This can be quite tricky if the links are small, for there is risk that the solder will run sufficiently to join two links immovably together. Very careful control of the flame is therefore necessary, and a minimum application of solder; the latter is best achieved by filing the strip of solder with a coarse file, then picking up a few grains at the end of the moistened borax brush and applying directly on the joint. The borax solution itself should be very thin.

Another aid to clean soldering is to construct a small stand of iron wire and suspend the link to be soldered from this, so that the joint is on top (22).

More elaborate links will need a jig of some kind to ensure that the shape is repeated exactly. This can be made by driving the ends of a few wire nails into a block of wood so as to form the appropriate design, and the wire is then wound round the nails (70). Using this method, however, it may not be possible to build up a whole coil before sawing. If the design is such that a single cut through the coil will be in the wrong place for alternate links, then the links will have to be made and cut one at a time: but it is surprising how quick even this can be.

Links can also be built up out of different elements soldered together, and these can themselves be formed on a rod or a jig. A simple example would be four round rings soldered together to form a rosette, but the possibilities are endless.

In working out a chain based on large or elaborate links, remember that it is usually not possible to join these together directly. Intermediate rings, known as jump rings, will be needed. These are usually small in order to set off the main links, and preferably oval or rectangular in shape. They may also be made of a lighter gauge wire.

Chain is by no means the only purpose for which wire is used. It can form the entire or the main constructional element in a piece of jewelry. The pendants shown

86

in the photographs(*35*, *128*), for instance, and the earrings(*77*) are made up entirely
of wires, having equal status with the stones which they display.

The construction of the earrings is illustrated(*71*). The upper two sketches show
how the 'tail' was built up, using 20 S.W.G. gold wire. When this was completed,
it was laid upper side down on a lead block and very slightly domed by tapping with
a ball-pein hammer. The centre sketches show the bezel and its base plate, the latter
with an extension to which the tail was subsequently soldered. A wire with a loop at
the end soldered at the junction between bezel and tails enables the piece to be attached
to an earscrew.

Wire can be applied to a base to add decorative elements, or even to constitute the
whole design. This was indeed a favourite procedure in the early days of the jeweller,
Far Eastern and Middle Eastern, Mediterranean, Germanic, Scandinavian, or Celtic.
The results in our museums are worth looking at. It was almost as if goldsmiths and
silversmiths, having discovered how to draw wire, could not tire of developing new
and more intricate and ingenious motifs.

What characterises these early works is not so much their ingenuity—that is to be

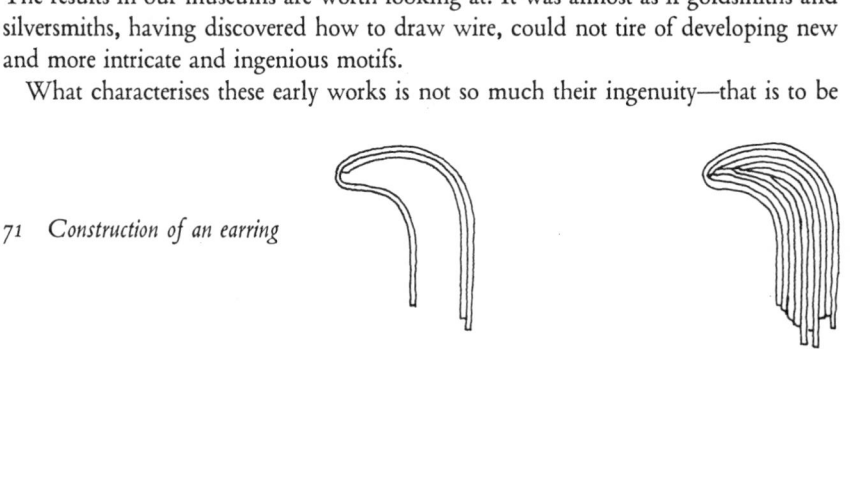

71  *Construction of an earring*

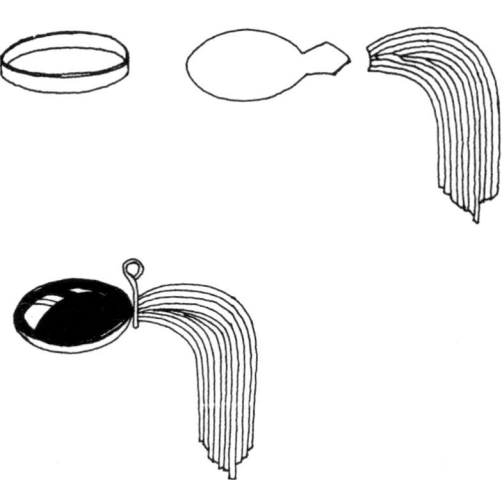

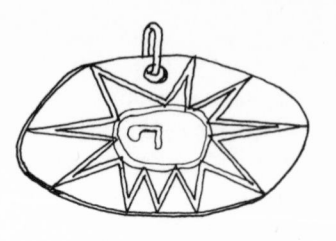

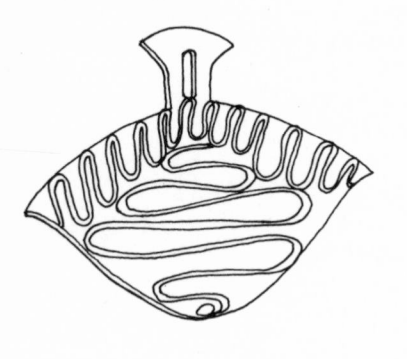

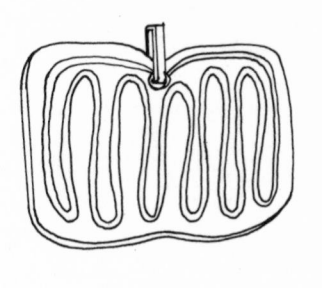

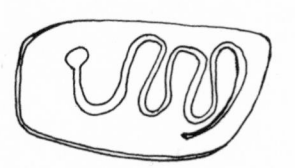

72 *Abstract designs in wire*
appliqué

expected from the creative mind—but above all their formalism. The discovery of modern art has been that there is just as much room for informalism. Much of present-day jewelry displays loose, abstract designs, and wire in loose, more or less abstract forms, soldered on to a plain base lends itself admirably to exploitation of this discovery. We illustrate various ideas, some based on the use of round wire, others on round wire hammered flat in places, or combined with other elements such as discs (72).

What we have described so far is wire used simply, but it can also be used twisted, either singly or as a combination of two or more wires; they may be of the same or of different sections, they may be just twisted together, or one may be twisted by itself and then twisted with another; they may be twisted left-handedly or right-handedly, or alternately one and the other. Once again there is no limit to the possibilities for experiment.

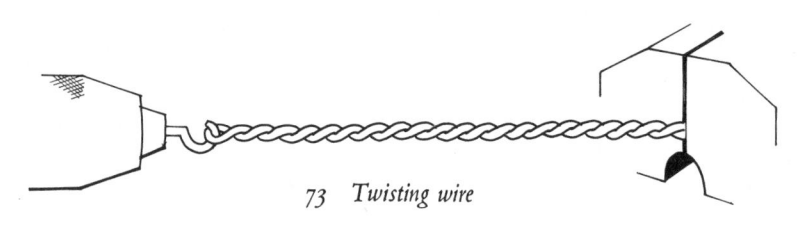

73 *Twisting wire*

The tools required are a vice and either a hand-drill or a hand vice (the former is faster working and ensures a more regular effect).

The technique is simple. Take a convenient length of wire (which, of course, should be well annealed), fasten one end in the vice, the other either in the drill or the hand vice, and twist.

If the same wire is to be used double, fold it in two, insert the open ends in the vice, grip the looped end in the hand vice or alternatively hook it with a cup-hook and secure this in the chuck of the drill, and twist (73). If different wires are to be used in

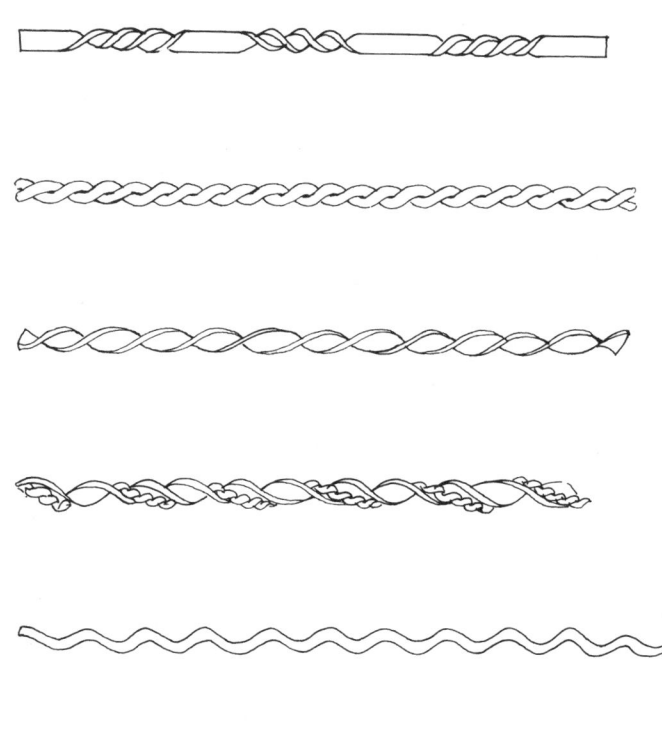

74 *Twisted wire forms*

combination, the same procedure is followed save that there will be no convenient loop, so that one will have to be formed by twisting the ends together.

Should you wish to alternate the direction of twist, the work will have to be done in sections, using the hand vice to grip the wire and moving it along as each section is completed. To ensure regularity you will, of course, have to move the hand vice precisely the same amount for each alternate section, and repeat the number of turns exactly.

The drawing (74) illustrates a few effects. The top wire is a single square wire twisted alternately to right and to left. The second wire consists of two round wires twisted together. The effect here—as indeed with all twisted wires—will vary very much according to the tightness of the turns put in. The third wire is a single rectangular wire. The fourth is a similar rectangular wire twisted and with two smaller round wires twisted together and wound into the rectangular wire. The fifth is two thick round wires twisted not too tightly, then separated. The sixth wire is a flat wire wound closely on to a round wire, which was then pulled out.

A final hint: since the possible variations are so numerous, and since they can always be repeated precisely, it will pay to keep a record of how each effect was achieved. This means noting not only the type and gauge of wire used, but also the number of turns given for any particular length.

The resultant wire can be given additional treatment either by being flattened with a hammer, or (after further annealing) by passing it through a drawplate. Every process will give it a new and individual character.

Finally the wire is cut into lengths, bent and shaped either to form a piece of jewelry, or to be soldered to another piece as a decorative motif; or if it is not too thick, it can be coiled and sawn to make up links for a chain.

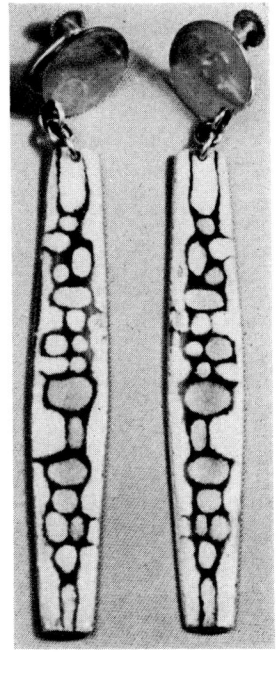

75 Enlargement of pendant shown in Fig. 67

76 Earrings, silver and enamel, by Gerda Flock-inger

77, 78 Earrings, gold and green cabochon tourmalines

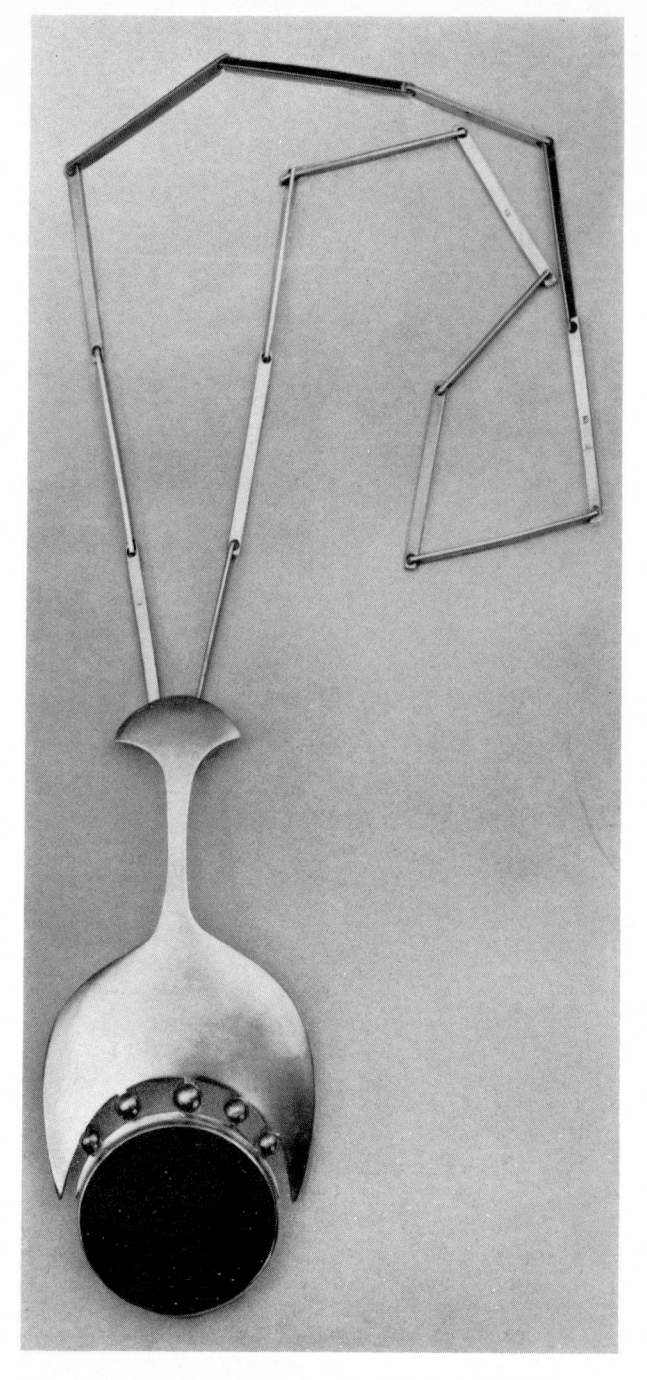

79 Pendant in matt silver and pebble by Helga Zahn

# CHAPTER IX

## *Fastenings*

Many forms of jewelry require fastenings of some kind: pins and catches for brooches, hooks or spring fasteners for earrings, hooks for necklaces. The perfectionist will make them all himself. The realist will know that such things are often very tedious to make and that he will do better to buy them ready-made: and jewellers' supply houses stock a big range of fastenings, which are known as 'findings', in base metal, silver, rolled gold and gold. They are not expensive. On the other hand, they are mass-produced and without individuality, so that in those cases where the fastening remains visible, as with a necklace, it is better to make one's own in keeping with the general design. In some cases where the fastening remains visible, but is of the simplest and most functional kind, as with an earring wire, it is probably better to buy, if only to save time and trouble.

### BROOCH-PINS

The simplest form of brooch-pin is made up of two rings having an internal diameter to fit the hinge pin(*80*). A flat is filed on each of the rings to enable it to stand upright and the rings are then placed in position parallel with each other on the back of the brooch and soldered on. This is fiddly and the rings have an irritating habit of moving or falling over as the heat is applied: it pays therefore to fix them in position while soldering with a simple V-clip of iron wire.

The pin is a suitable length of wire, one end filed to a point, the other bent to form a ring of the same internal diameter as the first two rings. The pin ring can be left unsoldered. To harden the pin and make it springy, the ring end is fixed in the vice and the pointed end gripped between pliers and given three or four twists, keeping the wire stretched as taut as possible.

The catch is made up preferably of square wire and soldered on to the brooch. Lastly the pin is fixed in position with a wire passed through the three rings, and the ends of the wire are spread by gentle tapping with a hammer and so riveted in position.

A neater variant(*81*) is made up as follows: Bend up a U of 10 B.M.G. strip

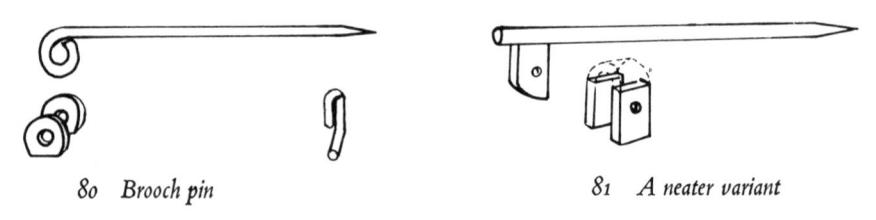

*80   Brooch pin*                              *81   A neater variant*

93

approximately ⅛ inch wide, with legs of the same length and spaced so as to provide a sliding fit for another strip about ⅛ inch square and of 12 or 14 B.M.G. metal. The U is soldered to the back of the brooch and a hole to accommodate the hinge pin drilled straight through the centre of both legs. The top of the U is then sawn or filed off and the corners are bevelled. The brooch-pin, of the same thickness as the little block (12 or 14 gauge), is then prepared, a groove to accommodate it filed along one edge of the block, and the two are soldered together so as to leave about ½ inch of tail projecting. This tail is fixed in the vice and the pin, gripped by pliers, given a few twists to harden it. The tail can then be sawn off, and the bottom rear corner of the block rounded by filing. Lastly, the block is set in position between its two supports and a hole to take the hinge pin drilled straight through the three pieces. The pin is fitted and riveted as before.

Commercially made pins are similar in design to that just described, but the catch is usually a safety catch fitted with a revolving slide which enables the opening to be closed, locking the pin in position.

In fitting a brooch-pin, remember that it should lie above the centre line of the brooch, for otherwise this will be top-heavy and will tend to lean forward.

## NECKLACE FASTENINGS

For ordinary chain used to hold a pendant  the commercial spring-bolt ring is perfectly suitable and can be obtained in a large range of sizes. Fixing it, however, needs care, for the spring actuating the bolt is very sensitive to heat, which ruins its temper. With a light chain it is best not to attempt to solder the link to which the bolt ring is attached; instead the open ends of the link are worked to and fro a few times to harden them and then carefully brought together to fit as closely and neatly as possible. With a heavy chain and ring, soldering can be attempted, using very easy solder and

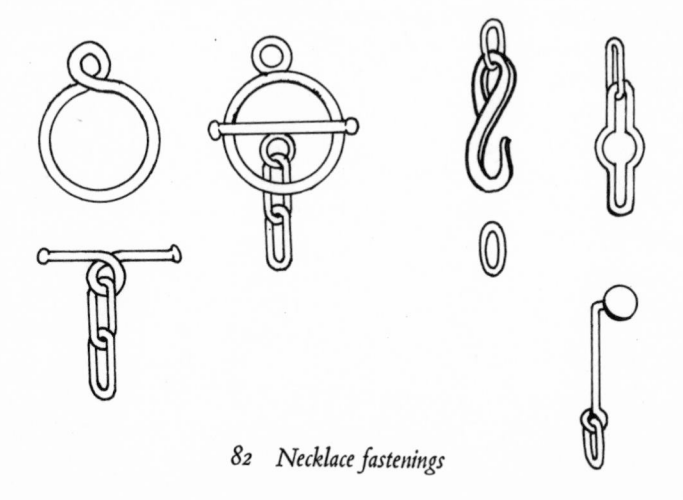

*82  Necklace fastenings*

protecting the ring as far as possible by wrapping round it a strip of newspaper soaked in water.

When the whole necklace has been specially designed, the simplest type of fastening is usually by hook and eye, but these too must be designed to be in keeping: if the necklace links are of wire, hook and eye must be of wire; if the links are of cut sheet, so too must be the fastening. And it is astonishing how the basic S-shape of the hook can be made to conform to the general design. A few ideas are shown (82), including an alternative to the hook, the bar fastening, which is one of the most secure fastenings known (though this is not to say that the hook is necessarily insecure).

Each end of the bar is decorated with a little ball. Hollow balls in silver and gold can be bought in a vast range of sizes, and soldered on. Here, however, it is simpler to cut the bar (of round or square wire) approximately ¼ inch longer than it is intended to be and to melt the ends. To do this dip the ends in borax, hold the bar vertically in a pair of tweezers, and apply the flame to the bottom end. As this melts it will thicken and become rounded. Continue the flame until the end has thickened up sufficiently, reverse the bar and repeat with the other end. Pickle. The resultant balls will probably not be quite perfect in shape because it is not possible to heat the metal evenly all round, but a little filing will true them up.

The obvious place for a necklace fastening is at the back, but it is often possible to avoid the obvious. How this is to be done will, of course, depend upon the piece, but three examples can be given (49, 15, 35). In figure 49, the fastening, hook and eye, is at one side and repeated in dummy form at the other; dummy because the hook is closed sufficiently to prevent disengagement. In figure 15 the fastening is embodied in the pendant. In figure 35 the necklace is a collar with no fastening at all.

## BRACELET AND BANGLE FASTENINGS

Bracelets which are essentially chain can be fastened like necklaces by some kind of hook-and-eye device. Again, it is important that this, being visible, should be an integral part of the design, as is illustrated (83, 107).

It will be seen that this bracelet consists of large links made up of pairs of strips ($\frac{3}{16}$ inch wide cut from 12 B.M.G. silver sheet) bent over at the centre and soldered

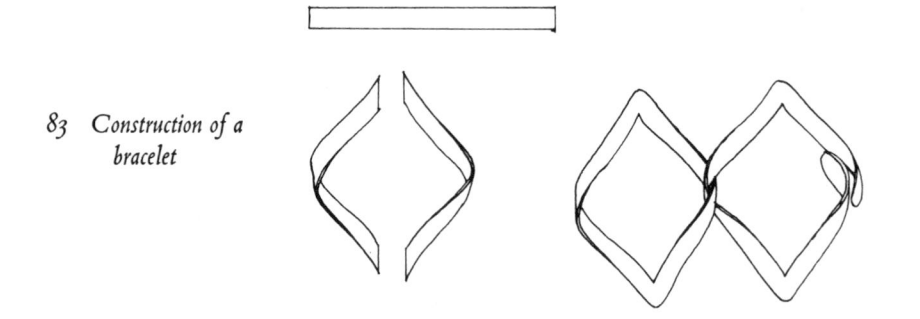

*83   Construction of a
      bracelet*

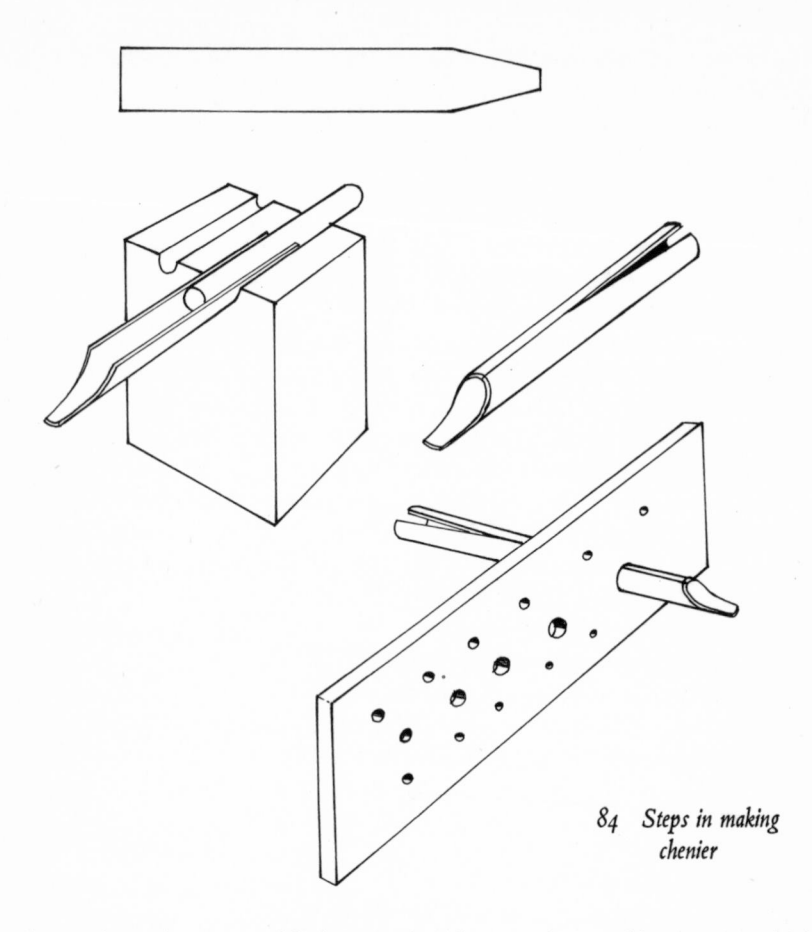

84　Steps in making
chenier

together at the ends. One end link is fitted with an oval ring of heavy wire which constitutes the eye. The other end link has open arms bent to shape and overlapping so that the ring can be slipped in and hooks over both with complete security (83).

Rigid or semi-rigid bangles and bracelets made up of two or more sections need different treatment. To begin with one or more hinges will be needed to join the sections.

The hinges are made up of *chenier* which is the name for fine tubing. The various steps in making this are illustrated (84). Cut a strip of 8 B.M.G. metal, ⅜ inch wide, which will produce a tube a shade under ⅛ inch in diameter (circumference = three times diameter plus thickness of metal). The edges must be quite straight and parallel. Taper off about ½ inch at one end. File a groove into the end grain of a block of hard wood, lay the strip on to this and hammer it in to produce a rough U-section. The proper tool for this is a light creasing hammer (85) the face of which ends in a narrow rounded edge; but it is perhaps safer to do the job by laying a length of thin steel rod, such as the shank of a twist drill, on top of the metal and hammering it in. If the sheet is too long for the groove, start forming at one end and move along as the forming proceeds. Finally hammer the edges over to make a rough tube; it does not matter if the edges do not meet, but they must not overlap.

We have suggested a block of hardwood to make a former, but it is also possible to buy a *swage block*, made of steel with a range of grooves of different diameters in its surface. This is a useful acquisition, but only if a fairly considerable amount of tubing is to be made for decorative purposes, for it is quite expensive.

Hammering the metal to form the tube will have hardened it, and annealing is therefore the next step. Now obtain some piano wire of the same diameter as the hinge pin is to be (in this case about 16 S.W.G.), grease and push into the tube. The wire should be somewhat longer than the tube, since the latter will stretch.

Insert the tapered end of the tube into a suitable hole in a round drawplate, and draw through. Repeat until the seam is properly closed. Now saw off the tapered end of the tube and pass the projecting end of wire through a hole in the drawplate big enough to take it, but not the tube, and pull the wire right out.

Cut off a section of tube the length of the width of the bangle sections, divide into three, and solder the tubes into grooves filed into the ends of the sections as shown (*86*). This must be very accurately done in order to ensure easy movement without binding and a neat appearance. In particular the tubes must be lined up exactly, and this calls for evenly filed grooves. A slight degree of misalignment can sometimes be corrected—if the thickness of the tube walls allow it—by putting the components together and passing a drill a fraction larger than the internal diameter right through the three sections.

85 *Creasing hammer*

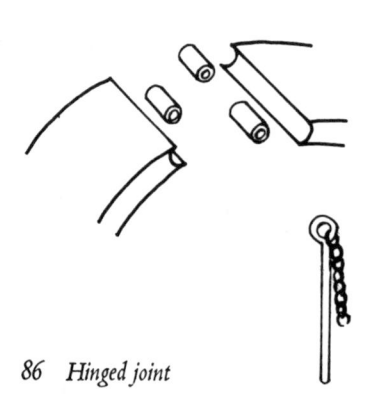

86 *Hinged joint*

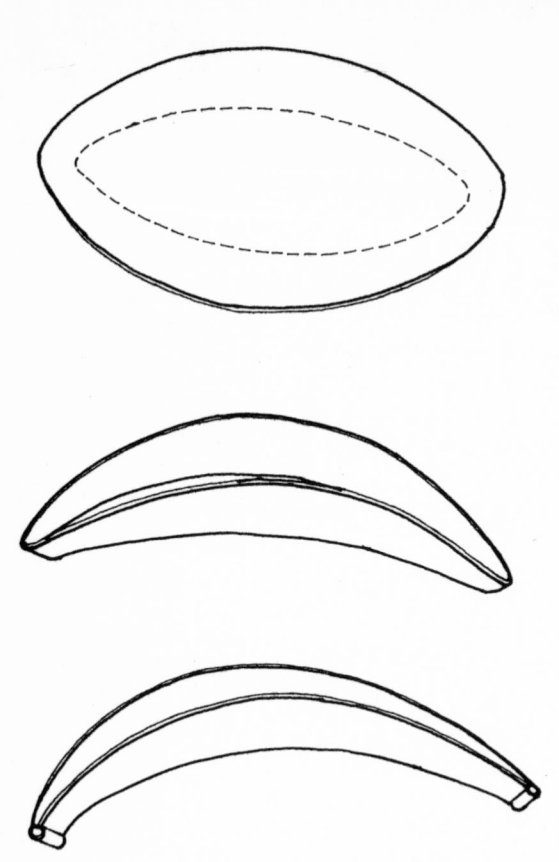

87, 88   *Construction of bangle*

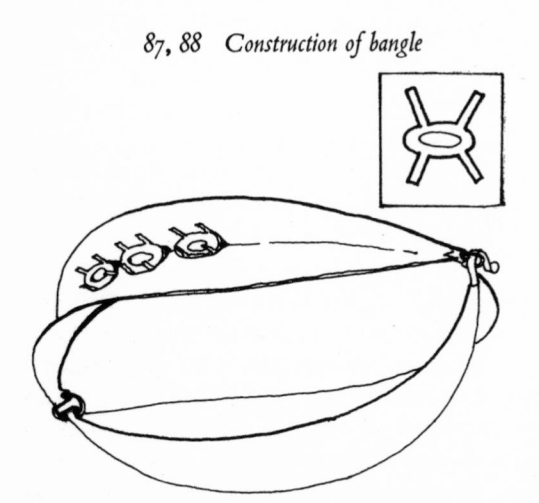

A hinge pin with the ends riveted over completes the joint.

The catch is made in precisely the same fashion, but is secured by a loose instead of a riveted pin. This pin should have a head formed on it and should be fastened to the bangle by means of a short length of safety chain.

If the ends of the bangle section are too narrow to allow a hinged joint of the kind described to be fitted, a more primitive arrangement can be adopted. This was used for the bangle shown (*109*), which is made of sheet copper, 10 B.M.G. subsequently gold-plated, and mounts three blister pearls.

The construction is illustrated (*87, 88*). Two oval shapes 4 inches long and $2\frac{1}{2}$ inches wide at the broadest point were cut out and their centres pierced as shown by the dotted line in the drawing (*87*). The shapes were folded in half so that the pierced edges met along their length but the outer edges remained separated. For neatness the pierced edges were first bevelled with a file and subsequently, after they had been brought together, the saw was run between them to ensure perfect mating, and they were soldered.

The next step was to make some fine chenier; this was soldered (after filing suitable grooves) to both ends of one section and one end of the other section. The remaining end of this section was fitted with a hook formed of a strip soldered at one end to the side of the section, then hammered to harden it and bent to shape.

Two oval links of round wire, one to hinge the two sections together, the other to fasten into the hook, complete the bangle.

The three blister pearls added as decoration are set in claws cut out of the same copper sheet in the shape shown (88), bent up and soldered in. In order to hold the irregular pearls more comfortably, the centre of the claw shapes was cut out and the shape made concave by a tap from a small ball-pein hammer, before soldering in.

## CUFF-LINKS

Cuff-links can be held together with chain, but this makes them more awkward to fasten into or take out of the shirt. The links shown in the photograph (110), of blue enamel and silver, avoid this difficulty and being rigid, ensure that the design is always presented from a particular aspect. This is a consideration if the design consists of, say, initials which should be seen the right way up.

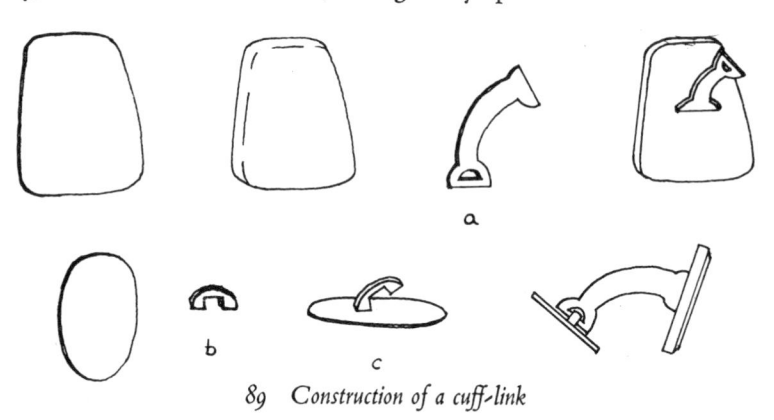

89   Construction of a cuff-link

a. arm; b. bridge; c. first step in fastening bridge

The construction is illustrated (89). The fastening is cut out of reasonably heavy metal, 12 B.M.G., to provide an adequate soldering base and to ensure that it does not become bent in use. An arm (a) is cut and pierced at one end; the other end is soldered to the front element of the cuff-links. This section will lie across the wrist and must therefore be set on the link in such a way that this presents its proper aspect.

A bridge (b) is cut and one end soldered to the near link. The other end is then bent up (c) just sufficiently to enable the pierced portion of the arm to be inserted. The raised end is pressed down again and soldered in position. It will be obvious that the base of the pierced portion of the arm must be no thicker than the opening in the bridge, so that it can swivel easily.

# CHAPTER X

## *Decorative Techniques*

The examples already given show how much may be achieved with the simplest imaginable tools and technique: saw and files for cutting and a modest degree of shaping, pliers for bending. However, even though modern taste encourages simplicity, there are times when something more elaborate is needed, particularly in the case of brooches and pendants not intended to be merely the setting for a stone, and which therefore depend for their effect entirely upon the manner in which the metal has been handled. This is not to say, of course, that more elaborate treatment will necessarily produce an object that *looks* more elaborate—it may in fact look more simple, some, thing well known in the dress fashion world where simplicity of line often conceals a wealth of sophistication.

The additional techniques available involve, broadly speaking, either surface treatment or shaping.

## SURFACE TREATMENT

On pp. 49–50 we have described metal colouring processes. To these can be added more or less informal texturing processes such as surface fusion and matting, and processes which produce a formal result, such as engraving and inlay.

### 1 *Surface Fusion*

If a soldering flame is played on sheet silver or gold, the whole piece will ultimately collapse and melt. If the sheet is not too thin, say 12 B.M.G. or thicker, it is possible with practice and care to melt just the surface of the metal, leaving the underlying portion unaffected, merely by whipping away the flame at the critical moment. The molten skin will set again immediately, leaving a surface no longer smooth but, literally, molten looking. The margin of time between surface fusion and collapse is only a fraction of a second, though obviously the thicker the metal the longer it will be. But this critical moment is not hard to assess, for the metal then suddenly develops a kind of intensely bright shimmer resulting from the fact that it is actually melting and moving.

The pattern that is created is informal and impossible to predict, though it can be controlled to a very slight extent. Thus if the flame is not applied evenly to the whole surface—and even application is extremely difficult to achieve because different portions of the flame have different temperatures—then the surface melting will not be even so that the molten effect will be more marked in one part than in another. This is something that can be used deliberately to intensify the effect in one part rather than

90 Ring, silver and blue cabochon stone

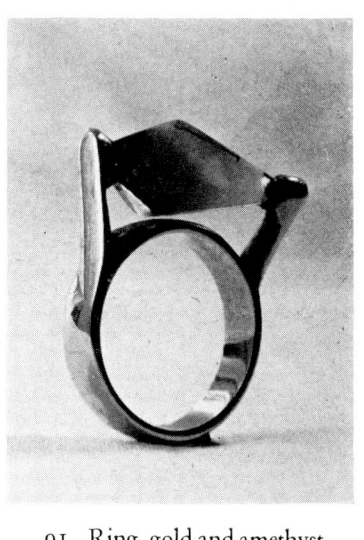

91 Ring, gold and amethyst

2 Collar and pendant, silver and brown
imbled agate

93 Enlargement of pendant shown on left

94 Pendant, silver and agates, by Kathleen Grant

another. Again, the effects will vary according to whether or not the surface is fluxed with borax, either all over or in parts.

An elaboration of this method is to place pieces of the same metal upon the piece being treated. Partial melting will then fuse these on. The pieces can be specially cut to a particular shape, or they can be accidentally shaped off-cuts, ends of wire, coarse filings and the like. They can be arranged to a design or scattered haphazardly. With this technique the result is easier to predict, but still only in the most general terms. All that is certain is that the texturing will be heavier than if no metal had been added, and that the sharp lines of the little pieces will be softened and lost, due to the partial melting.

## 2 Matting

A very controlled form of texturing can be achieved by the use of matting punches. Such punches have some kind of texture design indented in their faces (95). They are available in a wide variety, or they can be home-made out of short lengths (about 4–5 inches) of steel rod in one end of which, the face, the design is filed.

The metal to be treated is laid on a steel plate, and the punch applied and struck with a fairly light hammer so that the design is impressed upon its surface. The punch is then moved on and the process repeated.

A little practice on scrap metal is useful to enable one to judge exactly how heavy the blows should be so as to leave a clear impression, not so light that it is hardly visible, nor so heavy that the punch sinks right in; for the latter reason the metal should not be annealed. The other important point to watch out for is that the texturing should normally be even all over, which means that the punch-marks should touch so that no gap is left, but should not overlap, which would emphasise the line where they meet. And the hammer-blows must be as even as possible.

Punches, as mentioned, can be home-made without difficulty, but one can also dispense with them altogether. Again there is considerable scope for experiment. Thus a piece of fine wire-mesh can be placed on the sheet of metal and its design hammered in. Or a haphazard effect can be produced by scattering a little dust, quite thinly and more or less evenly, over the surface, and hammering *this* in. Dust contains a high proportion of irregular-shaped grains of silica, and they will leave their mark. Or nails with fairly large heads, such as the galvanised nails used for fastening roofing felt can be used instead of the punches, simply by impressing the irregular roughness on their heads. Or an old flat file can be laid upon the metal and hammered. For the ingenious the possibilities are unlimited.

95 Matting punches

## 3 *Engraving*

Engraving is a craft on its own, and a very highly skilled one at that. The difficulty is to achieve complete control of the tool, co-ordination of eye and hand. The technique itself is simple enough, and simple yet effective results are within the reach of the amateur.

The tools, known as gravers (*96*), are essentially chisels, short lengths of tempered steel rod of various sections, one end held in a wooden handle, wheel, ball or pear-shaped to suit individual preference and small enough to fit in the palm of the hand, the other end ground to a cutting edge.

Tool and handle are supplied separately and are fitted together by gripping the graver in the vice and hammering the handle on to the appropriate end with a mallet.

Gravers are obtainable in some eight or nine

*96    Graver*

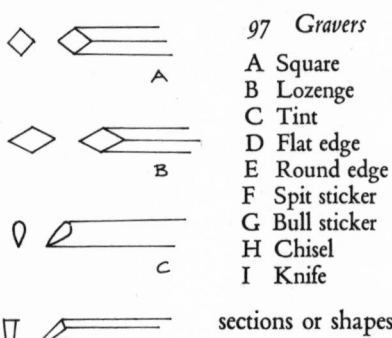

*97    Gravers*

A   Square
B   Lozenge
C   Tint
D   Flat edge
E   Round edge
F   Spit sticker
G   Bull sticker
H   Chisel
I   Knife

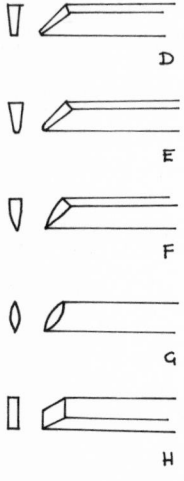

sections or shapes, each in about half a dozen sizes. They are illustrated (*97*). For engraving fine lines, e.g. to texture a surface, you will need a square (A) and a lozenge (B) or a tint graver (C). For wider lines, and for carving out a whole surface, flat edge (D) and a round edge (E). These two shapes are also known as *scorpers*. For general carving, a spit sticker (F) or a bull sticker (G). The chisel (H) is similar to the flat edge, save that its sides are parallel. The knife (I) is similar to the lozenge, but cuts finer lines.

In use the graver is held with the fingers pressing against one side (not curled round underneath), the thumb laid along the other side, and the handle comfortably cradled in the palm of the hand. The point of the graver should not project more than $\frac{1}{2}-\frac{3}{4}$ inch beyond the thumb. If too long, as is usually the case with new gravers, the excess length can be snapped off with pliers; if this proves too difficult, grip the graver (without its handle) in the vice so that just the excess length projects from the jaws, and break by striking a smart blow with a hammer.

The thumb itself not only completes the grip but—and this is very important—its tip is pressed against the other thumb, or the edge of the work or some convenient adjacent surface where it not only steadies the hand but acts as a brake, preventing the graver from slipping—with possible injury to the other hand—and enabling it to be stopped at precisely the point desired.

Gravers must be sharp and ground to the correct cutting angle, which is 45°. A bigger angle will tend to make it dig in, so that it becomes impossible to push forward, or alternatively to slip. A smaller angle is liable to break.

Sharpening should be carried out by rubbing the face of the tool on a medium carborundum oilstone, and finished on an 'Arkansas' stone, using a thin machine oil. The Arkansas stone, which is a very hard, fine-grained natural stone will produce a mirror polish on the face and a superlative edge. It is in fact a hone.

In sharpening the face must be kept flat on the stone, and the edge must not be bevelled (which would alter the cutting angle) or rounded. The wire edge, or *arris* which is left is removed by sticking the point of the tool once or twice into a piece of wood, the leg of the work-bench for instance.

If the graver is to be used for work on concave surfaces the portion underneath the face, the 'heel' of the tool, must also be ground away (98); this will affect the lie of the face, since the cutting edge of 45° must still be retained.

Grinding and honing are tedious processes, and honing must be repeated not infrequently during actual work, since the edge becomes blunted fairly quickly in metal. If you happen to have an electric grinding wheel available, it will pay to grind off the top front inch or so of the tool, so as to remove approximately half the face, leaving only a relatively small area to be sharpened (98). When doing this, however, be careful not to let the tool become too hot, as it can do very quickly, for this will destroy the temper.

The professional engraver will have quite elaborate equipment for holding the work while he operates, but for amateur purposes this is not necessary. Obtain a small block of wood 2–3 inches square and melt on to this a layer of sealing-wax. For flat work $\frac{1}{4}$ inch thick will do. Warm up the wax to soften it, press in the work-piece so that it is gripped all round, and allow to set.

Holding the block firmly on the table with one hand, apply the point of the graver with the handle fairly high, press forward gently and lower the handle. The edge of the tool will first catch, then as the handle comes down and the correct cutting angle is reached, it will slide forward making its cut.

Practise a series of short straight lines to begin with, with a square or diamond-shaped graver, following lightly scribed guide lines if you wish, until you have gained the feel of the tool and can do this quite confidently. Do not forget to steady

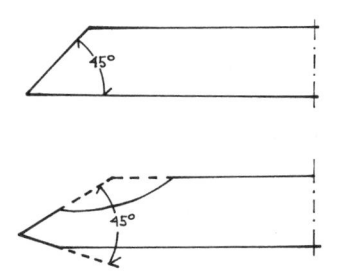

98  *Graver cutting angle*

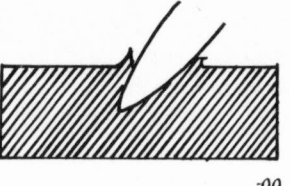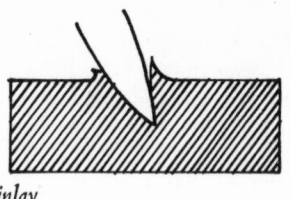

·99   *Grooving for inlay*

the hand by pressing the thumb against the edge of the block or the thumb on the other hand.

The graving will raise a thread of metal which should curl vertically upwards; if it curls to one side, this means that the graver is lying over to that side and should be straightened. At the end of the stroke the curl is simply jerked off with an upward flick of the point of the tool.

Curved lines are executed in the same way with the graver pressing forward in a straight line. To achieve the curve it is the work-piece that is turned, using the other hand. Practise this too, starting with gentle curves until you can engrave a tight perfect circle.

When you have mastered the square or diamond graver, try some of the other shapes to see what different effects you can produce.

The graver can be used both for incising a design, texturing a surface, and for carving. For the beginner, it is texturing that will be the most important. Try covering a surface with graved lines parallel to each other and so close together that they practically touch. This is the essence, but very varied effects can be obtained in the application. Try lines about an inch long and compare the effect produced by very short lines, no more than ⅛ inch or so, or even 'stitches' produced merely by digging in the point and lifting it slightly. Create patterns of whorls like fingerprints, touching but set at different angles to each other. See the difference between deeply engraved lines and shallow ones, thick lines and those produced by the finest tint tool. Each method will have its own character, depending upon the subtle interaction between reflected light and shadow created by the many tiny planes which the graver will cut.

## 4 Inlay

Inlay is an adaptation of engraving and consists in carving out grooves or areas in the surface of the work-piece and filling these with a different coloured metal.

Grooves are filled with wire. The metal, which for inlaying purposes should be reasonably thick, say 12 B.M.G., has a deep groove cut in it with two cuts of the diamond graver or, better, the spit sticker or bull sticker. The tool must be tilted to one side in the first cut, to the other in the second cut, so as to form an undercut on each side (99). The groove must be absolutely regular in width at the top or difficulties may result when the wire comes to be laid.

Draw some wire, round or rectangular, so that it fits the groove exactly in width, but is a little thicker than its depth so that the wire will project a fraction when inlaid.

100   *Wire inlay*

Anneal and insert. Hammer in, using a hammer with a slightly rounded face or even a ball-faced hammer, so that the wire is driven and spread into the undercut which will hold it(*100*). The hammering must be carefully done. A slight tilt of the face, or a blow which lands at the side instead of on the wire, will leave a mark which only considerable filing will remove. Smooth off with a flat hammer such as a planishing hammer(*102*), then file and smooth the whole surface level.

Area inlays are executed in a somewhat similar manner. For this it is best to begin by cutting out of thin sheet the design to be inlaid. Place this on the work-piece and

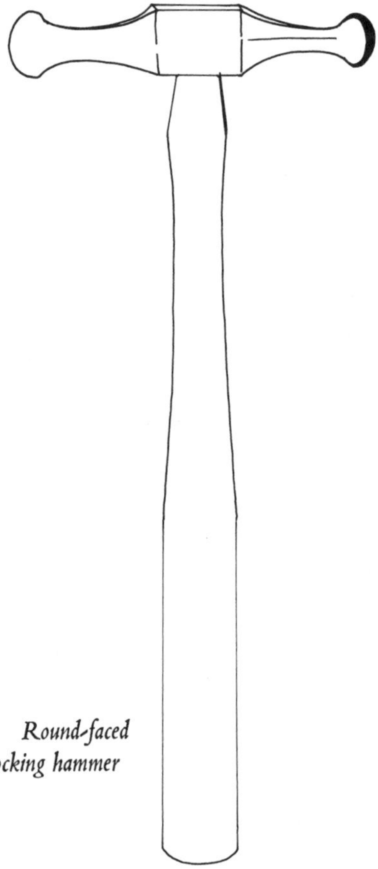

101   *Round-faced blocking hammer*

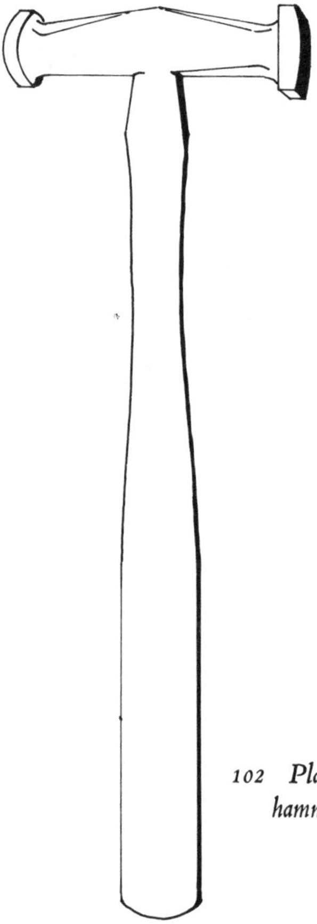

102   *Planishing hammer*

107

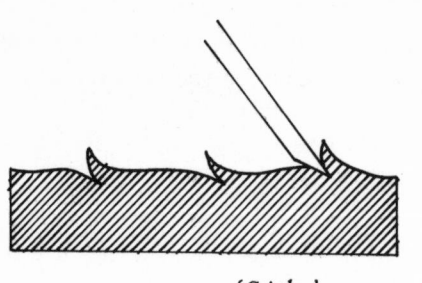

*103* 'Stitches'

trace its outline with a scriber. With a flat-edge or chisel graver, carve a level recess a little less deep than the thickness of the inlay, taking care to work inside the scribed outline which, of course, will be a fraction larger than the inlay. The object is to achieve a perfect fit.

The edges of the recess must be under-cut as before with the bull sticker. Now work a series of 'stitches' (*103*) all over the floor of the recess by digging in the point of the square graver and lifting the handle so as to raise a short spike. These stitches will become embedded in the centre portion of the inlay and will thus serve as a key.

Anneal the inlay, set in position and hammer as before. If you have a small block of smooth polished steel which can be placed so as to cover the whole inlay, the hammering process will leave no marks at all.

Finally, file, stone smooth and polish.

There is an easier method for working the recess needed for area inlay. This consists in cutting the outline of the inlay out of another sheet of the base metal, slightly thinner than the inlay, and soldering this on to the base. The edges will have to be undercut and stitches raised as before. Some people might consider this method less craftsman-like than the other, almost cheating in fact; but it works, and certainly it ensures an absolutely level base for the inlay.

The inlays described have all assumed that the metal to be inlaid is softer than the base metal. If this happens not to be so, then the result of hammering will be to distort the base rather than to force the inlay into the undercuts. In such a case the inlay will have to be soldered in position. This is best done by covering the floor of the recess or the underneath part of the inlay with a thin surface of solder, setting the inlay in position and re-flushing the joint so that the solder shows all along the edges. Obviously the solder in such a case must be of the same colour as either the inlay or the base metal, so that the solder line will not ultimately show as such.

## SHAPING

So far we have shaped sheet only by bending with pliers or by hand, or by hammer-ing with a rawhide mallet on to a former such as a ring triblet. It is possible also to shape with a steel hammer, with or without the use of special shaped punches. In all cases the work must be supported, and usually, moreover, supported by some substance with a certain amount of 'give'; for the result of hammering on to a solid surface, of steel for instance, would be to thin and stretch the metal. The support is provided either by pitch or by a lead cake.

To prepare the pitch, heat up 1 lb. of Swedish pitch but do not boil. When fluid stir in about ¼ lb. of powdered resin, then 1½ lb. of plaster of Paris, and lastly a lump of tallow about the size of a walnut or a little more. All this must be well mixed, then poured into a shallow wooden box, such as a cigar-box, and allowed to set. The mixture must be hard and tough, but not brittle. For winter use, a little more tallow can be added.

The ring shown in the photograph (*90*), setting a large blue cabochon stone, was made as follows. A rectangular piece of paper (1) was cut, its length (a) equal to the circumference of the stone, and its width (b) equal to the intended height with sufficient allowance for the shank (*104*). The paper was folded in four (2) and one corner cut out as shown in (3) where the length (c) represents the height of the ring above the shank. The opened paper formed a template (4) for cutting out a piece of silver sheet 10 B.M.G. The sheet was rounded on a triblet to a cylindrical shape and the edges (c) soldered in order to enable the shape to be trued up. Next an inverted V was cut out at the joint and the edges resoldered. The legs, too, were rounded up to form a ring shank of the correct size, and soldered (5).

Now for the shaping. A lump of pitch, softened, was pushed into the ring so as to fill it completely, and left to set. When hard, the ring was hammered evenly all round with a narrow ball-faced hammer, very gently at the top, somewhat harder lower

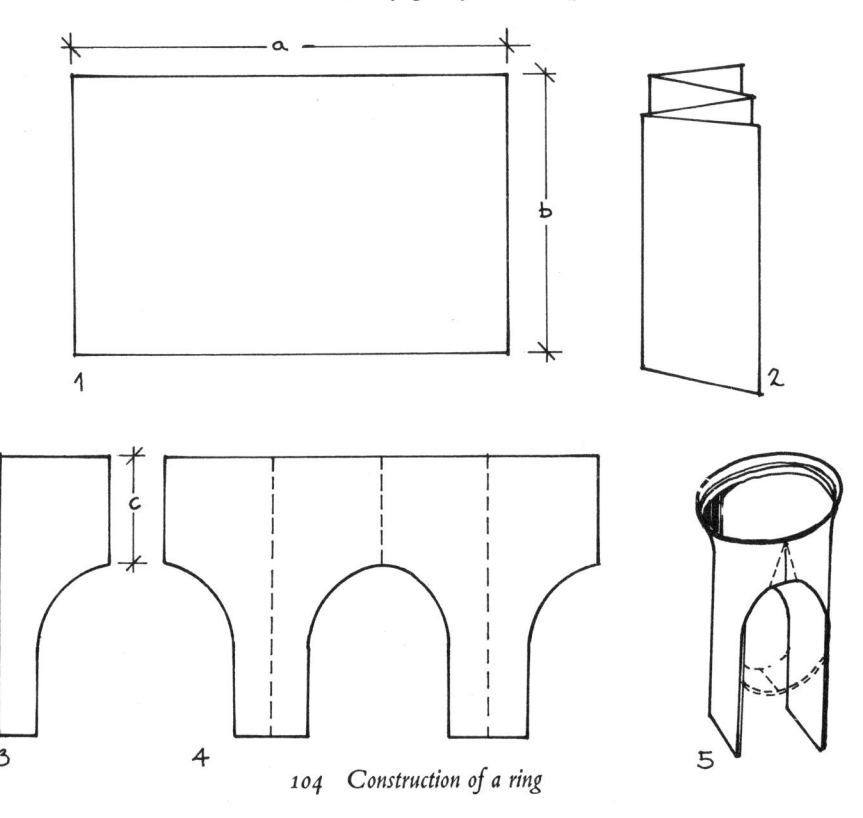

*104  Construction of a ring*

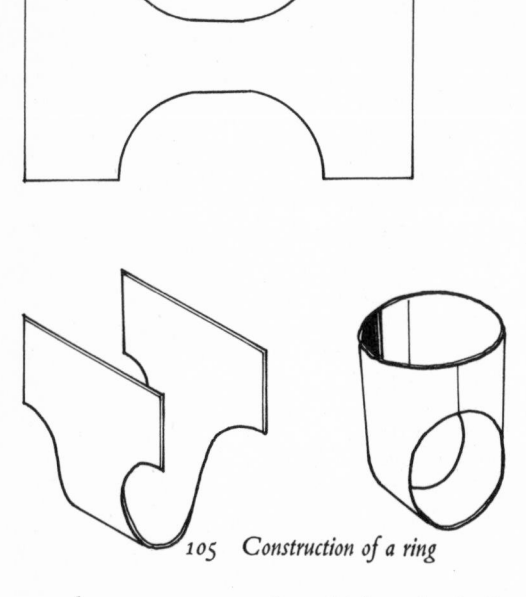

down as far as the finger open‑ing, so as to produce a curved taper. To prevent distortion while this was being done, the ring was held in the hand rest‑ing for support on the table, and the ring was constantly rotated so that the blows were applied closely in concentric rings with the blows more or less touching, but not over‑lapping.

Lastly a bearer was fitted in the top and the stone mounted.

This method is particularly useful for irregular‑shaped stones, such as the one shown in the photograph (90), but an alternative method is offered (105); this is suitable mainly for regular‑shaped stones, whether round, square or rectangular, which need to be lined up with the shank. The drawing is self‑explanatory and it will be seen that the upper portion has two pairs of edges to be soldered, and the V‑shaped cut will have to be taken out of each of these.

*105   Construction of a ring*

A refinement which can be added in either case for greater comfort in wear, is to make a tube with an opening equal to the ring size, and solder this into the ring shank so as to close off its upper portion. The shank should, of course, have been made big enough to allow for this.

The technique described can be applied to any hollow shape, but the modelling possible is obviously limited. For working flat sheet, and for more elaborate designs, steel modelling punches are needed (106). These are available with faces of many different shapes and sizes, square, oblong, round, triangular and either flat or more or less rounded. Some have very narrow, chisel‑like faces; they are known as *tracers* and are used to outline the design.

The work that is done with punches is known as *repoussé*, when the design is punched out from the back to form a raised surface on the front, and *chasing*, which is the sharpening and texturing of the design working on the front of the metal.

Take a piece of sheet, 8 B.M.G., with a simple design traced upon it. Warm the surface of the pitch gently with the flame, being careful not to burn it, and press the sheet in so that it is firmly gripped at the edges. There must be no hollow spaces underneath for the metal needs to be supported all over. The design must be on top so that it can be seen.

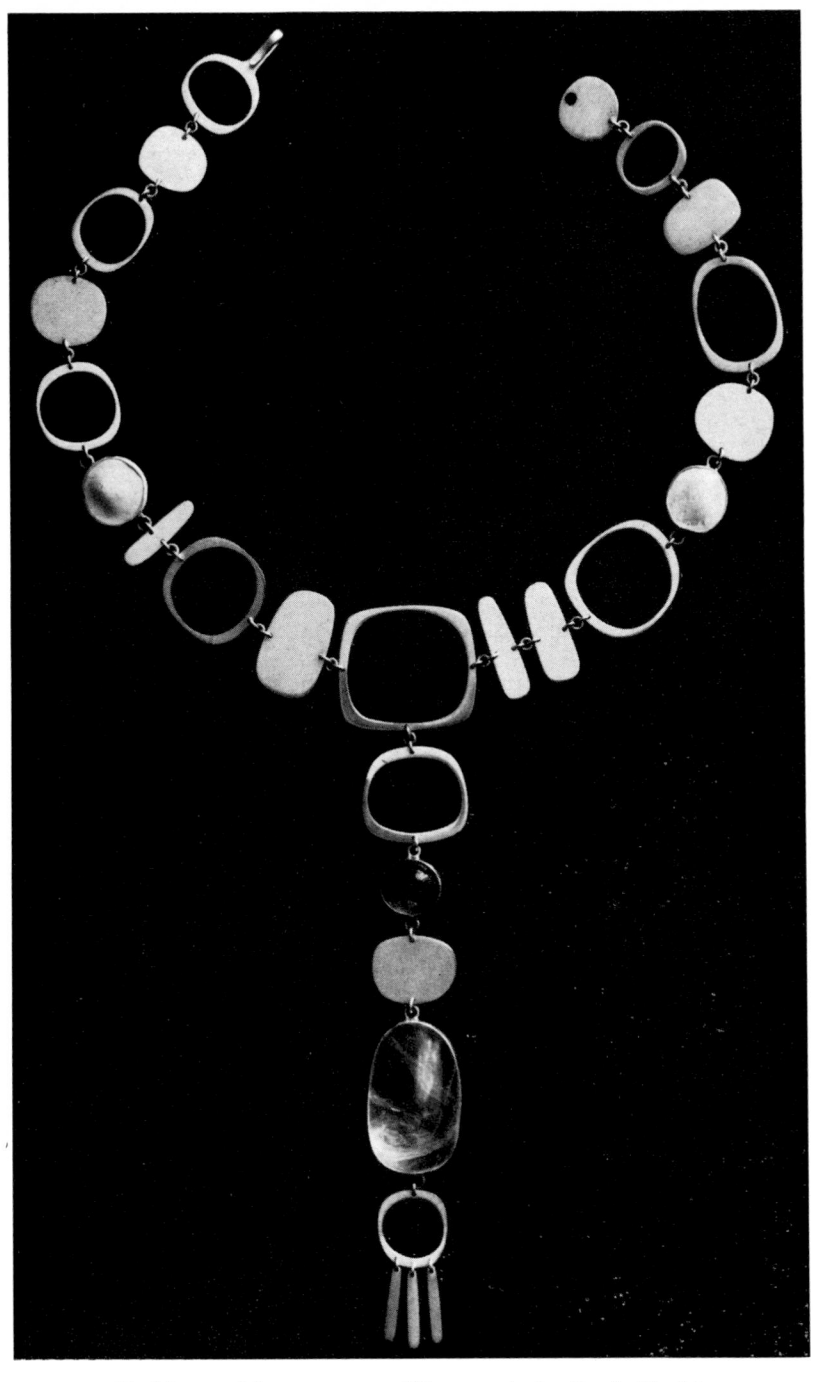

106  Necklace, gold, moonstones, blister pearls, by Gerda Flockinger

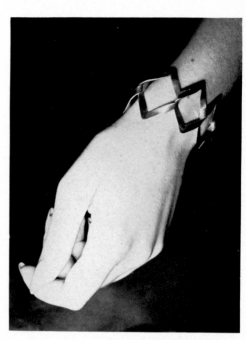

107 Silver bracelet

108 Collar and pendant, blue cabochon stone and blue and green enamels

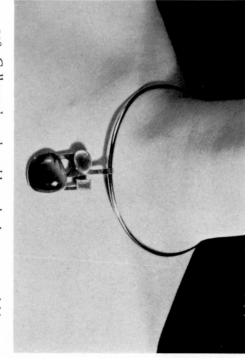

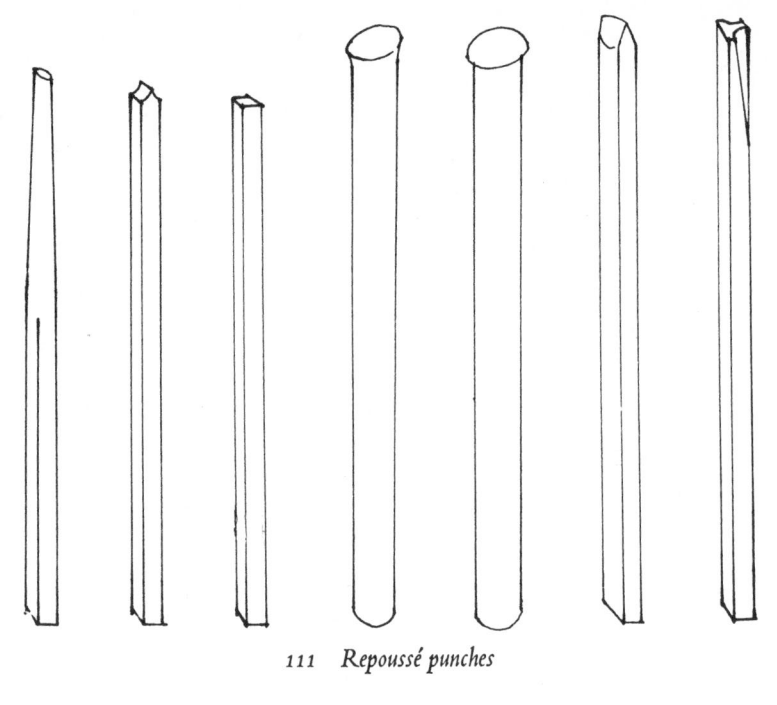

111   *Repoussé punches*

When the pitch has set again, start by outlining the design with the tracer. The tool should be held resting on and in line with the traced line of the design, with the handle tilted slightly away from you. The edge of the hand holding the tool rests on the pitch-block, so as to ensure control, and moves the tool along as it is struck with a rapid succession of blows from a light hammer, preferably a chasing hammer (112), which is specially balanced for this work.

The blows need not be heavy, but progress must be smooth and continuous to ensure an even smooth line. The work is best done if the pitch-block is so positioned that the punch is constantly travelling towards you, though, of course, this will not be possible on a curve when the punch must be kept turning.

When the outline has been completed, the work should be pried loose from the pitch and cleaned up, either by wiping any pitch which adheres with a rag dipped in paraffin, or by burning. The design should now appear clearly as a raised line on the other side of the metal. If too faint, or otherwise unsatisfactory, the process must be repeated.

Now anneal the metal, replace on the pitch with the raised design on top, and work the areas in between with a suitable modelling punch. These areas will become raised areas on the other side, which will be the right side. The punch or punches chosen will depend on the shape and depth of modelling required, a flat-faced punch for low relief, a rounded one for deeper modelling. This time the punches are not tilted but are kept straight upright, though constantly moving as before so that the modelling remains smooth and even, with nicely flowing transition from low parts to high parts.

When the repoussé is completed, remove the work again, clean, anneal and replace, this time right side up for finishing. It is very important now to ensure that the modelled hollows are properly filled with pitch. If necessary this can be done by melting pitch into them and allowing this to set before the work is replaced.

The finishing process consists in sharpening up the outlines of the modelled design and smoothing the background areas with suitably shaped flat or slightly convex punches.

Repoussé lends itself to the most elaborate designs imaginable. Hunting scenes, Last Suppers, gods and goddesses, all these were favourite subjects when the taste of wealthy patrons ran towards the rococo. We admire often, but seldom wish to emulate. Fortunately the pitch-bowl and the punch can serve less fanciful tastes equally well.

If the shape is to be very simple, the lead cake will probably serve. This is home-made. Obtain some lead: scrap such as old electric cable sheathing will do perfectly well. Melt this in an iron saucepan, and when molten pour into a rectangular tin or even a wooden box measuring approximately 5 × 3 inches, and 1–2 inches deep. Be careful not to pour the dross which will have formed a kind of skin on the surface of the liquid lead.

When the cake has cooled off, shake it out of the

*112   Chasing hammer*

box and it is ready for use. The process is a kind of primitive repoussé, using modelling punches, but omitting the first tracing stage and the final tooling. It is therefore suitable only for simple doming and grooving. It is often helpful to pre-shape the block by beating a suitable depression in it with a ball hammer (113).

The doming can be carried

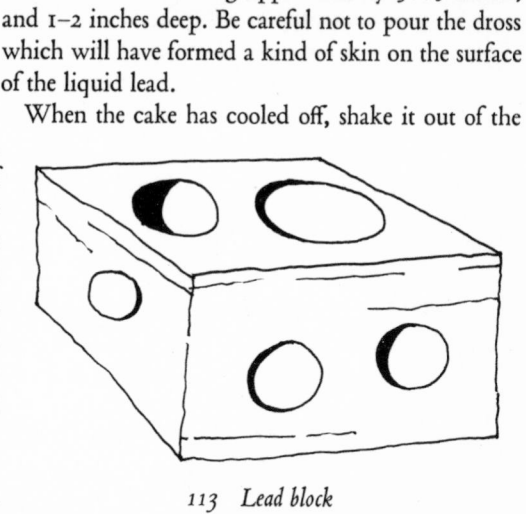

*113   Lead block*

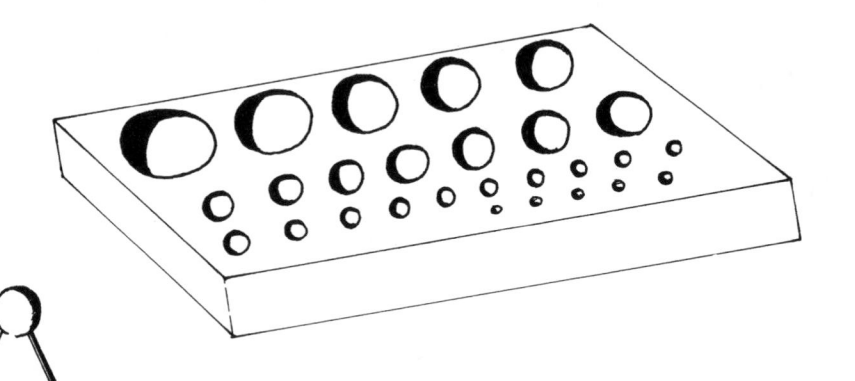

114, 115 *Doming punch and block*

rather further by investing in a set of doming punches(*114*), punches
with ball-shaped heads graduated in size from approximately $\frac{1}{8}$–$\frac{9}{16}$ inch
diameter, and available in steel or in wood. Select a punch of the size
desired and hammer it into the lead cake to form a corresponding
depression. Cut out a circle of thin sheet, lay it over the depression and
drive it in with the punch. This will produce a perfectly shaped hemi-
sphere, though the edges will need truing up.

Domes of this kind can be soldered on to surfaces as a decoration, or
they can be soldered together in pairs to make beads.

If it is intended to make many such domes, it may pay to obtain also
a doming-block(*115*), a steel or brass block with the corresponding holes
to take the place of the lead cake; and a set of cutting punches(*116*),
which enable circles of the correct size to be punched out of the metal.
Such punches are really cutters, and their edges must be treated gently.
When cutting, therefore, lay your sheet on the lead cake, and not on the
steel block, before driving the punch through.

Lead has an unfortunate effect on silver when heated with it: it eats
its way in like a bad case of rust in iron. Consequently when silver has
been worked on the lead cake it should always be cleaned very carefully
with fine emery paper to make sure that no trace of lead remains; only
then is it safe to solder. But prevention being better than cure, it is in any
case always advisable to place one or two sheets of paper between silver
(or gold) and lead before working.

116 *Cutting punch*

# CHAPTER XI

## *Enamelling*

Enamelling is a very ancient art form, dating back at least 2000 years. Its earliest appearance is as a glaze on clay bricks, but already by Greek and Roman classical times a technique had been developed for fusing coloured glazes on to metal, thus enabling enamelled jewelry to be produced. There was need for it since although stones could be and were used to introduce colour, the lapidary had not yet raised his skill to the point where he could facet or impart the high polish needed to make the stone show to best advantage.

Enamelled jewelry is still popular for the brilliance of its colours which exceeds that of any stone.

Five main techniques for applying enamels are in use at the present time, known by their French names which, it is said, have been handed down from the eleventh century. They are *Limoges*, *Cloisonné*, *Champlevé*, *Basse-Taille* and *Plique-à-jour*.

Of them *Cloisonné* is believed to be the earliest. The name comes from the French word *cloison*, meaning 'enclosure'. In this process narrow flat wires are soldered in a pattern on to a base, the spaces in between forming enclosures which are filled with enamel to the top of the wires. The tops of the wires remain visible and serve not only to separate the different colours but also to outline them, just as patches of colour are outlined in a stained glass window.

In *plique-à-jour* this technique is carried a step further, by dispensing with the backing material while retaining the cloisons. The enamels used are always transparent, and the light passing through produces an effect which is exactly that of a stained glass window in miniature.

For *champlevé*—the word means 'raised field'—hollows carved out of the surface to form a pattern are completely filled with enamel which, as in the case of cloisonné, is usually opaque enamels. Colour and metal surround are both of equal importance in the design, and it is this which distinguishes champlevé from basse-taille.

*Basse-taille*, meaning low cut, actually employs a technique similar to that of champlevé, but in a much more advanced form. Recesses to hold the enamel are cut, but in these recesses there is carved in addition a pattern of figures, flowers or animals in low relief, about $\frac{1}{80}$ inch below the overall surface of the metals. Transparent enamels are then fused into the recesses, and being transparent they will allow the carved pattern to show. But not only this; since the carving varies in depth, there will be variations in the thickness of the overlying enamel resulting in variation in depth of colour and producing the most subtle and exciting gradations.

The processes described all involve filling in recesses with enamel. The *Limoges*

116

technique, so called after the town in France where it was extensively practised and perfected in the fifteenth century, does not rely upon cloisons or carved-out cells. It is in fact a painting process demanding a high standard of draughtsmanship from the enameller. The base was usually a plate of copper, very slightly domed. A layer of opaque white is fused over the entire surface and the scene to be depicted outlined in black oxide or finely ground enamel which is then fired. Gradually the picture is built up with the colours required, plenty of opaque white being used as well as plenty of shading. Each step is fired, so that as many as twenty firings might be needed to complete the picture; and for each step the whole surface is coated with a very thin layer of enamel so that the surface always remains even. The last step is always a coating of clear enamel to give depth to the picture.

A feature of Limoges enamels is that they were always *counter-enamelled*, i.e. enamelled on the back to prevent distortion and cracking, whereas this is rare in champlevé.

Limoges enamels are executed in naturalistic colouring, but the technique gave rise to a variant, also calling for a very high degree of skill in draughtsmanship, known as *grisaille*. On a background of black or very dark enamel some pictorial scene is represented built up in white with delicate black lines and shading. Great attention was paid to anatomical detail of figures, both human and animal. The result is certainly grisaille, meaning greyishness, but the word does not in any way convey the extremely striking three-dimensional chiaroscuro effect achieved by the French master enamellers.

117  *Mortar and pestle*

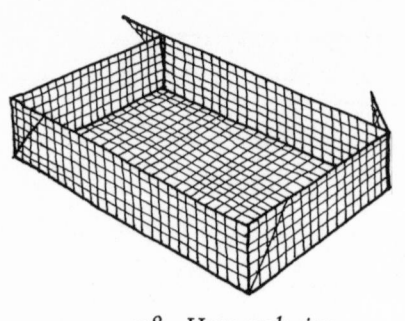

118 *Home-made sieve*

There are relatively few nowadays who practise Limoges and grisaille, or even true champlevé and basse-taille, for the time such work takes makes the product expensive. The modern commercial equivalent of champlevé and basse-taille involves laying transparent enamels on an engraved, often engine-turned, background pattern. In addition a great deal of experimental work is done in what must be called the brutal manner, its outlook and results utterly divorced from the delicate work of past centuries. We discuss this later.

Enamel is a kind of glass of fused silica (flint or sand), red lead and soda or potash. The lead and potash give it greater elasticity than ordinary glass possesses, and enable it to withstand high temperatures. The lead in addition, by penetrating the surface of metals on which the enamel is melted, allows this to fuse with the metal and adhere.

The compound, which is colourless and transparent like glass, forms a substance called *flux* (this has no connection with the flux used in soldering!). Metallic oxides and salts can be added to this to produce coloured enamels, either transparent, opaque or opalescent. Flux or the coloured enamels can be bought in slab form or, more normally, broken into lumps known as *frit*.

The process of enamelling, very briefly, is to pound the lumps of enamel into a fine powder, using a mortar and pestle (*117*). The powder is washed until it is absolutely clean, and is then applied, either wet or dry, to a prepared metal surface and fused by being brought to a bright red heat.

For the workshop, then, you will need a selection of enamels, opaque and trans-parent, say 2 ounces each, stored in small bottles or jars with lids. Also a Wedgwood mortar (5 inches diameter is a convenient size) and pestle. A small agate pestle and mortar, such as chemists use, is extremely useful for final grinding, but somewhat expensive.

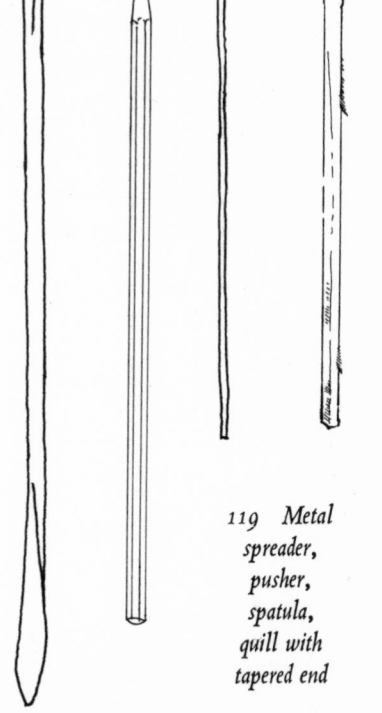

119 *Metal spreader, pusher, spatula, quill with tapered end*

118

*120   Glass brush*

For grading the powdered enamels, and for scattering them over the work, a sieve of 60 mesh and one of 80; if you prefer you can buy a few square inches of brass or copper mesh and bend this to a box-shape which will serve equally well (*118*).

For applying the enamels a few feather quills, a home-made metal spreader and a spatula (*119*), a couple of sable brushes, medium, an ordinary paint brush, and some gum tragacanth.

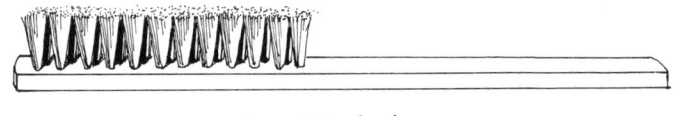

*121   Wire brush*

For cleaning up surfaces a ½ inch glass brush (*120*), a long handled wire brush (*121*), some fine steel wool, and coarse, medium and fine carborundum stone, ½ inch square. Sulphuric acid, 10 per cent, will also be needed, and pure nitric acid (though this is not essential).

For supporting the work while it is being fired, some stands and supports made as required of stainless steel sheet or wire, say 16 S.W.G. These supports will probably need to be specially designed for each job, and a selection is shown (*122–5*).

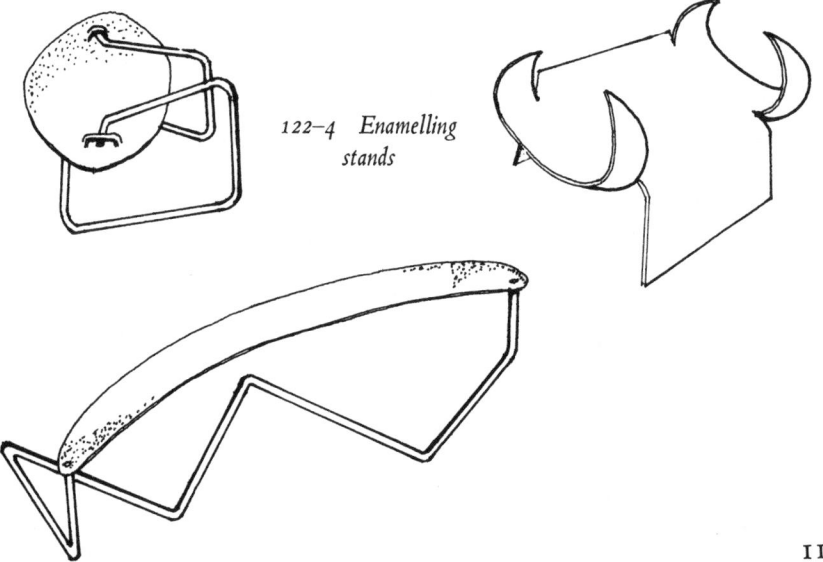

*122–4   Enamelling stands*

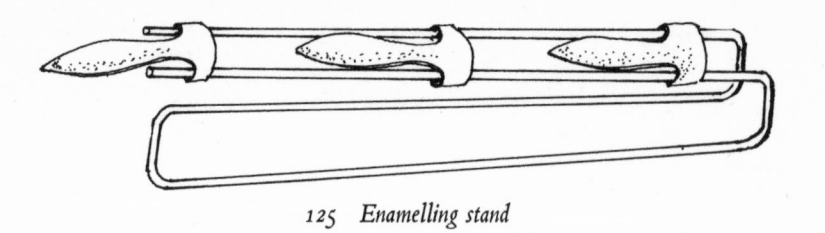

*125   Enamelling stand*

Lastly, the heating unit. An electrical kiln with temperature control is the ideal, but this is quite expensive and not really justified unless you are going to enamel on a fairly considerable scale. The much more modest, but very effective alternative is a home-made muffle.

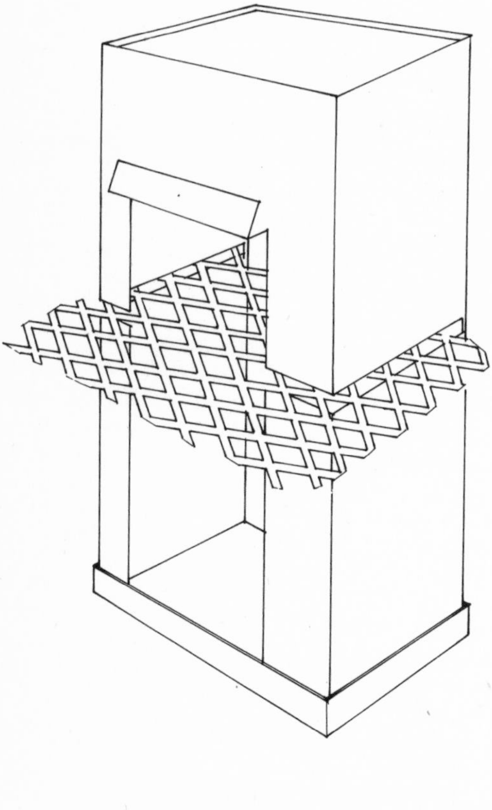

*126   Home-made muffle*

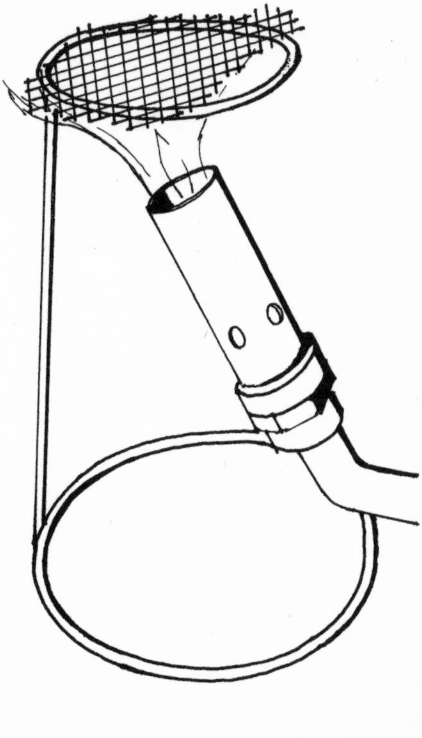

*127   Open stand for enamelling*

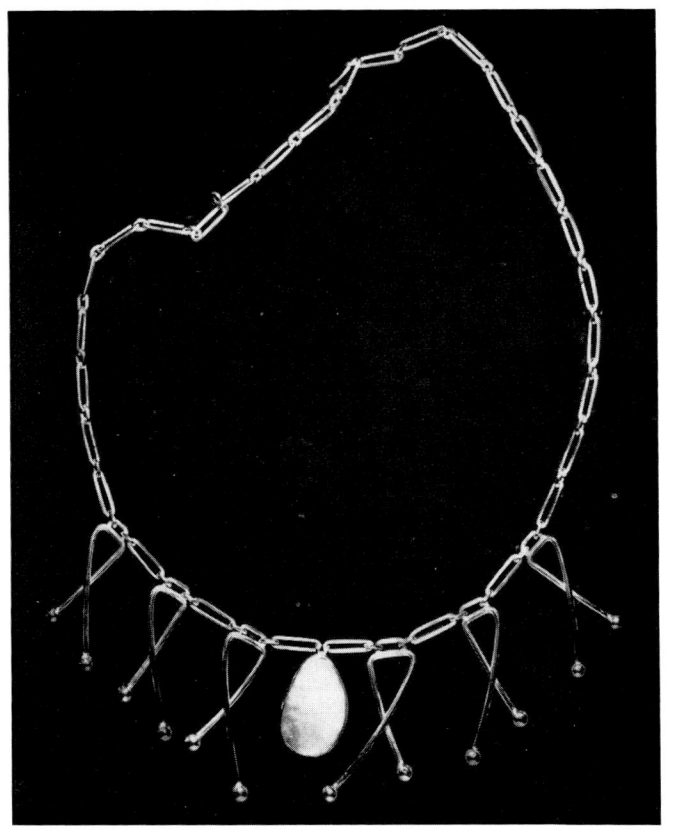

128 Necklace, silver gilt
and green cabochon stone

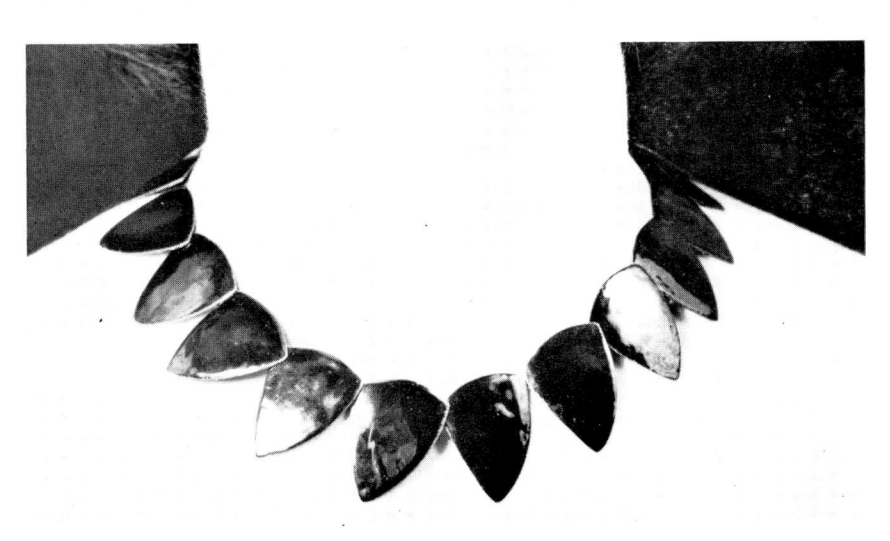

129 Necklace, copper with black enamel

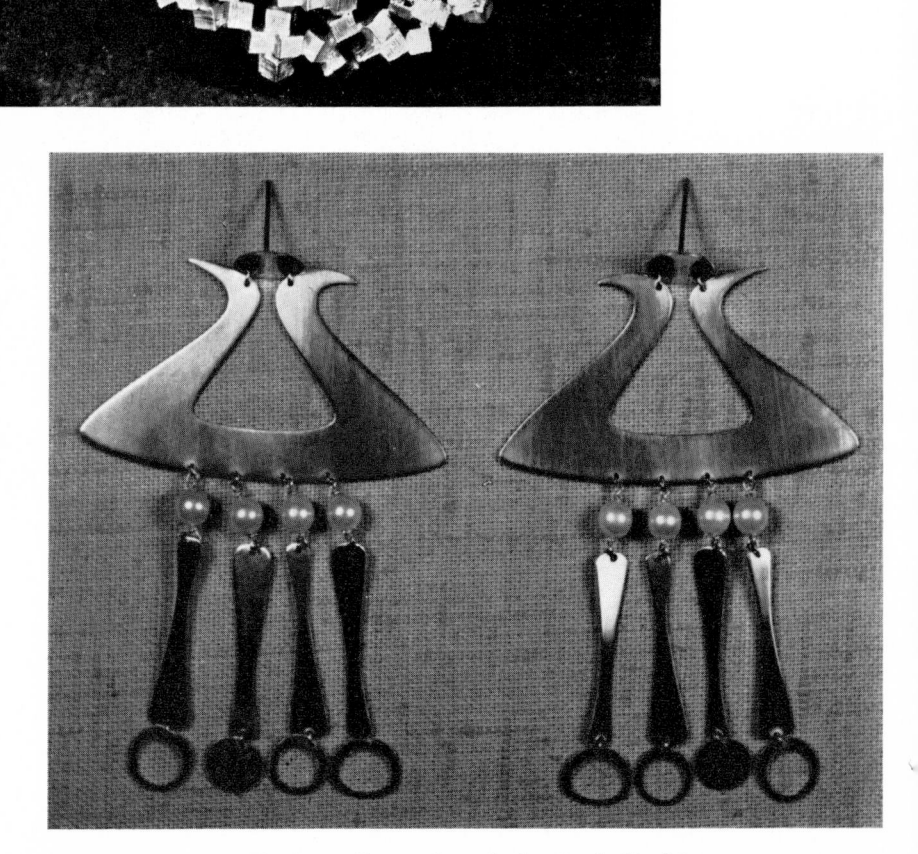

130 Pendant brooch, gold, diamonds by John Donald

131 Earrings, silver and pearls, by Gerda Flockinger

For this you will need a rectangular tin with lid, measuring about 12 inches high, 6 inches wide and 4 inches deep. Working from the top downwards, about two-thirds of the front is cut out, and the sharp edges left are turned over to avoid any risk of injury. A slit about $\frac{1}{2}$ inch wide is cut in each side, about half-way down. These slits support a tray made of stout gauge expanded metal such as is used in the building trade as a foundation for plaster work.

The drawing (*126*) shows the completed muffle, and it will be seen that the tin has been up-ended and stands on its own lid. A great deal of heat will be involved, so the tin should be placed on a couple of blocks of asbestos or, safer still, the kitchen stove.

The heat is provided by bottled gas—butane or propane—feeding one of the larger-size burners available, which is held by hand projecting into the tin through the opening below the tray. The work to be enamelled rests on a stand made of stainless steel wire bent to shape, which in turn rests on the tray. The upper portion of the muffle serves the same purpose as the kiln: it retains the heat and, above all, ensures top heat which speeds up the fusing of the enamel.

As a matter of fact even a simple muffle such as we have described is not essential. It is possible to rest the piece to be enamelled merely on a tray of expanded metal placed on a stand, and apply the heat from underneath (*127*). But the resultant loss of heat renders the process slow and unreliable, so that this method is really suitable only for very small pieces.

## METALS

Copper is a favourite metal for enamelling on. It takes enamel well, it is cheap, it does not melt when over fired, and it will stand up to almost any kind of rough treatment. Gilding metal is perhaps even better. It has all the advantages of copper except its softness: this makes it somewhat harder to work, but on the other hand it retains its shape better when heated.

The supreme metal for enamelling is gold, 18 carat or better, and a special alloy which is free from zinc is available. It does not oxidise or discolour when fired. It can stand extreme heat, and there is no need to worry about specks of fire oxide flying off and getting buried in the enamel, as may happen with copper. Lastly, though gold is a soft metal the application of enamel adds sufficiently to its strength for it to keep its shape.

Gold is particularly suitable for transparent enamels, especially reds. The British Museum has a magnificent specimen, the so-called King's Cup, made in France about 1380.

Silver, too, is a fine metal for enamelling, particularly suitable for the transparent greens and blues. One must be very careful not to overheat, however, for then there is considerable risk of melting the piece. This renders silver less suitable for use with certain very hard-firing enamels, where the margin between fusing temperature and melting-point is small.

For this reason it is safer in such cases to use fine silver, which has a higher melting-point than sterling. Since, however, fine silver is too soft to stand up to reasonable wear and tear, it is best to enamel only small pieces that can then be treated as gem-stones and set in a bezel.

The silver and gold we have discussed have been the solid metals. The same rich effects can, however, be achieved by applying them in the form of foils to copper or gilding metal and fusing transparent enamels over these.

Silver and gold foils are hand-beaten from the pure metal into sheets so thin as to be almost transparent. They are sold in a standard size of 3 inches square. Each foil is put up between two layers of tissue-paper and should be handled between these because it is too flimsy to manage without such support. The foils are usually sold annealed, but it is as well to make sure of this when buying, for otherwise you may find that it crinkles up uncontrollably when you apply the heat.

Foils are always used in small cut-out shapes which are known as *paillons*. Draw the outline on the tissue paper, then place these (with the foil between them) on several layers of blotting-paper and with a very fine needle prick holes all over the shape. This is done in order to allow air and steam to escape from under the paillon when fired, but can be omitted if the paillon is very small. There should be something like 100–150 holes per square inch of foil, and if a very fine needle is used they will not show after firing. The task can be speeded up by sticking a dozen needles or so into a large cork, leaving about $\frac{1}{4}$ inch of point projecting (132).

The paillon, still between the tissues, can now be cut out with sharp scissors and allowed to fall into a bowl of water, where the tissues will float off.

Paillons are not applied directly on the metal base, but on to a layer of enamel, flux or coloured, which has been previously fused, then coated with gum tragacanth.

Pick the paillon out of the water with tweezers and place in position, pressing down with a piece of blotting-paper to squeeze out any air bubbles and excess gum.

The next step is to fire. This fuses the foil into the underlying enamel and must be done carefully for the foils, being so very thin, are easily burnt and will then have to be stoned off completely. The firing process should be interrupted several times so that the piece can be taken out of the muffle and the paillons gently burnished to smooth them down.

Enamelling then proceeds in the normal fashion, one or more layers of enamel being added to cover the paillons.

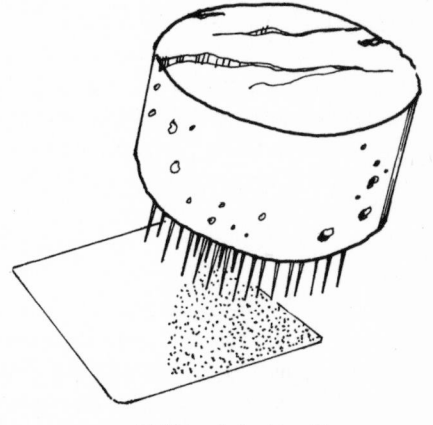

132   *Pricking holes in paillons*

# PREPARING THE METALS

The metal to be used must be thoroughly annealed to reduce the risk of distortion while firing, which would not only spoil the shape but is likely also to cause the enamel to crack off. To anneal, bring to a dull red heat, then cool as described in Chapter I for the various metals.

Cleanliness is vital. The piece must now be pickled. Copper and gilding metal should be boiled for a few minutes in a 10 per cent sulphuric acid solution in a copper pan. Silver should be dipped and re-dipped in slightly warm pure nitric acid until all trace of blackening has disappeared leaving a matt silver surface. Gold is pickled in a 10 per cent solution of nitric acid, warmed. Nitric acid is very powerful, so never leave a piece in it for any length of time or the surface will be attacked and eaten away. Neither at this stage nor subsequently should the piece be handled with fingers for these would leave a greasy film. Brass tweezers should be used for dipping in sulphuric acid, glass tongs for handling in nitric acid: if no glass tongs are available, suspend the piece from a hook made of silver wire. After pickling, silver or gold pieces should be brushed with the glass brush under running water, and copper or gilding metal can be given a brisk rub with a brass-wire brush, also under running water.

Nitric acid deserves a special word of warning for it is very powerful, and in addition the pure acid gives off fumes harmful to the lungs. It needs to be treated with even more respect than sulphuric acid. When diluting it, remember as in the case of sulphuric acid to add it slowly to the water, and not the other way round. The mixture will in any case become extremely hot, but if the water is added to the acid, the reaction causes spitting which may splash hot acid where it is least wanted, on hands or face for instance.

After cleaning, all metals should be burnished with an agate or steel burnisher dipped in water. This gives an extra smooth and bright surface particularly good for transparent enamels. Moreover, the burnishing, by closing the pores of the metal reduces the risk of air bubbles adhering during the firing and becoming embedded in the enamel.

When the piece is burnished it can be dropped into a bowl of water and left until you are ready to enamel. Copper and gilding metal can be given one further treatment immediately before applying the enamel. Gentle heating in the muffle will bring them to a peacock iridescent colour—*gorge de pigeon*—which, under flux, produces strange chance patterns in rich tones of red, green and brown. The iridescence is in fact a light film of oxide which contaminates and colours the flux.

Silver and gold need no cleaning between firings, but copper and gilding metal, whose uncovered portions will suffer heavy oxidation, must be pickled between firings.

# THE ENAMELS

Enamels are available in a wide range of colours, clear and opaque. The beginner should limit himself to five or six of each, in addition to colourless flux. Even a limited selection will give plenty of scope for they can be used in thick or thin layers, on different materials, in different colour arrangements, or one colour fused over another.

The following may be suggested for a start: 2 ounces each of transparent pale blue, dark blue, pale turquoise, green, ivy green and red; opaque dark lapis lazuli, turquoise, soft-firing white, emerald, orange and soft-firing carbon black; and lastly a medium flux. Colour charts are unfortunately hardly ever obtainable, being no doubt very expensive to produce. One must therefore rely in the first instance on the manufacturers' list of names: they are an approximate guide only, and, moreover, the same names from different manufacturers are liable to produce different results.

It will pay to make test pieces using different metals, and to keep a careful record of how the particular effects were achieved. Only thus is it possible to repeat them at will.

One important characteristic to note is that different enamels fuse at different temperatures. It is this which is referred to when they are described as hard and soft firing, meaning high and low temperature fusing. Soft enamels may burn if subjected to as much heat as hard enamels need for fusing. Transparent reds in particular are fugitive so that the colour disappears altogether if they are overheated. For this reason, if several enamels are to be applied one must start with the hard ones and follow up with the soft. Not only is this necessary for reasons of temperature, but if a hard enamel is laid on a soft one the latter will bubble up, causing the hard enamel to look spotty and to crack away.

Fluxes, too, are supplied in different grades. They are particularly effective as an underglaze for transparent coloured enamels on copper or gilding metal, producing a much more brilliant effect than if the colour is laid directly on the metal; and as a very thin final overglaze to protect from wear. But in any case the same work principle applies: a hard flux under a hard transparent; a medium or soft flux under a soft colour, and a soft flux as overglaze.

Enamels cannot be mixed to produce different colours or shades. The grains of powder remain separate when fused, producing a speckled appearance which, of course, can be used, but only as a special effect. Variation of shade or tone can be achieved by laying one colour over another, with separate firings, but the scope here is fairly limited.

## PREPARING THE ENAMELS

While enamels can be obtained in powder form, this is hardly worth while because the powder does not keep well; it will in any case require washing before it can be used. It is best, therefore, to start with frit, and if the lumps are too big to be convenient they can be broken quite easily by heating with the torch, then dropping them into a bowl of cold water.

Put a few lumps into the mortar, cover with water and grind until they are reduced to grains the size of fine sand. This is a rather tedious process. While it is being done the enamel should be washed frequently in changes of water. Fill the mortar about a third full under the cold tap, swirl around, leave about 10 seconds for the enamel to settle, then pour off the excess water and continue grinding. The water will be milky in appearance, which is caused partly by impurities in the enamel, but partly also by material from the mortar itself. This is the reason why it is best to finish grinding in an agate mortar which, being much harder than the enamel, will not be ground away. Practice will teach you how fine to grind. Opaques need more grinding than trans- parents, being usually harder firing. Transparent enamels if ground too fine tend to give trouble with air bubbles. Within limits the coarser the grind, the more brilliant the finish; but if the grind is too coarse, then the enamel will not cover the surface well nor will it flow readily in firing, so that the final result will be pitted. The 60 or 80 mesh sieve is recommended for ordinary purposes, but for painting delicate grisaille work and the like, the powder may have to be as fine as 200 mesh, which is the texture of flour. When the enamel is ground sufficiently fine it should be washed in seven or eight changes of water; this is particularly important for transparent enamels where the water from the last couple of rinses must come out absolutely clear. Finally the ground enamel should be put into a small dish (133) and covered with water until needed; this will protect it from dust. If stored in water in a stoppered bottle it will keep for 6–8 weeks but must then be re-ground and washed before use.

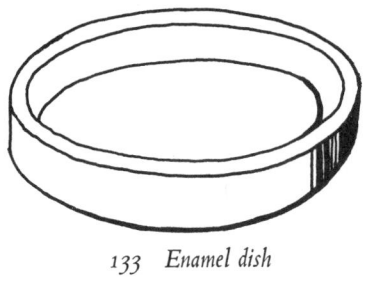

*133 Enamel dish*

## APPLYING THE ENAMEL

The process of applying the enamel is known as *charging*, and it can be done with the enamel dry or wet.

To dry the powder it can be put on a sheet of blotting-paper placed on an electric warm-plate or the top of an electric fire. The disadvantage is that however careful one may be, some dust is bound to get in even if the powder is covered. On the other hand it can be applied more thinly and evenly, scattering the powder from a sieve of 60 or 80 mesh screen, or a little basket bent up out of this material. Using this method, and interposing little shapes cut out of thin cardboard, it is also possible to stencil, as it were, a design on to the work-piece.

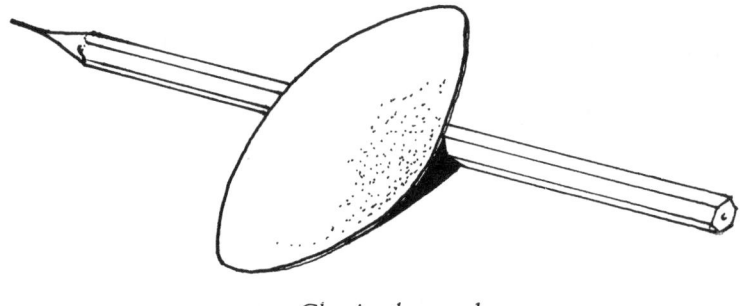

*134 Charging the enamel*

In order that the powder may adhere, the work-piece should first be painted with a solution of gum tragacanth bought from the chemist. The work-piece should rest on some small stand such as a pencil on a clean sheet of paper (*134*). It can then be picked up more easily, and any powder spilt on the paper can be poured back into its container. Edges of the piece which are not intended to be enamelled can be cleaned up with the tip of a moistened paint brush. When all is ready the work-piece is carefully lifted by inserting the flat end of the spreader underneath, and placed on its stand ready for firing.

When applying the enamel wet, drain off most of the water in the dish containing the enamel and prop it up on one side so that it stays tilted. Taper the end of a turkey or goose quill (*119*), obtainable in craft shops, and use this to scoop up the enamel, a little at a time, and spread it on the surface. The moisture should be just sufficient for easy flowing, but not overflowing. This is a matter that practice will get right: if too wet, the enamel will run off the surface, and if too dry it will cake in lumps. If the surface of the metal is domed, mix a little gum tragacanth solution with the enamel to help it adhere.

Now touch a soft clean cloth or piece of blotting-paper against the sides of the metal so as to soak up as much moisture as possible and place the piece on top of the muffle to help it dry out completely while the muffle is being pre-heated. The enamel must not be too wet for as the heat reaches it the water will bubble and displace the enamel. When the enamel is dry, it will be quite light in colour and no more steam will rise from it. Cunynghame, author of the classic work in English on enamelling (see Bibliography) was very meticulous on the subject: 'Dryness may be tested by holding over it a piece of cold, transparent window glass, and noticing whether any moisture is deposited upon it—in fact just the same plan as is adopted by prudent persons at an inn to see if the beds are damp.'

Charging requires experience—and patience—to get just right. The coatings should always be thin, two thin coats separately fired being better than one thick one which is almost certain to crack when cooling off. When enamelling on copper or gilding metal, however, be particularly careful that the layer, though thin, really does cover all over with no bare spots: these would oxidise and blacken in the firing with great risk that some specks of fire scale might fly off and become embedded in the enamel. Silver does not raise this problem and it is quite easy to add enamel to any patches left uncovered and then re-fire.

When the piece is charged, inspect it carefully to make sure that the enamel is only where it is meant to be. If any has strayed on to adjacent portions or edges, pick it off with the tip of a damp paint brush.

## FIRING

Firing may be done in an electric kiln, the home-made muffle we have described, or in the open over a flame from the torch.

The temperatures required to fuse enamels are high, ranging from about 1200°F to 1600° F, with opaque enamels normally harder firing than the transparent. These factors must be borne in mind. Silver, for instance, melts at about 1500° F and cannot therefore be used with enamel which has a higher melting-point than this. Enamelling solder has a range of approximately 1350–1450° F, which is lower than that of many enamels. This does not mean that soldered pieces cannot be enamelled, but it does mean that the design must be such that the piece will not fall apart if the solder melts. It means also, in the case of transparent enamels, that it must be used very sparingly and kept as far as possible from the surfaces to be enamelled; for it will certainly melt and may then spread under the enamel and show up as a silvery patch.

Firing in the open is the simplest method. It requires no more than a stand, a bunsen burner stand for instance such as can be bought from dealers in laboratory equipment, and on this a tray of heavy expanded metal (127). The tray should be painted with a paste of rouge powder and water which will prevent fire scale from flying off on to the enamel. The article is placed on the tray and heat applied from underneath, by blow-torch or bunsen burner, very gently to begin with then intensely until the enamel melts completely, with no sign of bubbles or graininess. This is judged by eye. When the enamel is thus fused, remove the heat instantly.

This is all that is required; it sounds, and is primitive, but perhaps we may once again quote Cunynghame: 'Lastly I would venture to call the attention of ladies to the pretty things they can make out of gold and enamel with no other tools than scissors, pliers, a few jeweller's files, and a spirit-lamp and blowpipe. Such charming things as enamelled ships, birds and animals, which were so beautifully done in the 16th century, and which we justly admire in the museums, are easy to make by the whitest of fingers in the most tidy of drawing rooms.'

Kiln and muffle are similar, the difference being efficiency. With the kiln there is no guesswork in heating, for this is controlled and evenly distributed; and little loss of heat, for the kiln is insulated. The muffle lacks both these advantages. For these reasons the muffle is not suitable for pieces larger than 1–2 square inches, rings and similar articles in which the enamelled surface is not on top.

Handling procedure, however, is similar.

Iron trays and stands should be painted with rouge powder and water as a guard against fire scale, and this applies also to the inside of the muffle which otherwise will form a great deal of it.

With a kiln the article is not put in until fusing temperature has been reached. A muffle also has to be pre-heated, the point being that the more quickly the enamel is melted, the brighter the result. This pre-heating is particularly important when re-firing enamelled copper or gilding metal, for the enamel will always crack from the heat before it melts and flows again, and if the cracks should appear while the muffle is still fairly cool, they may stay open long enough for the metal to oxidise and produce black pits and lines in the enamel.

The piece to be fired should also be pre-heated, but very gently to prevent warping and distortion of the metal. This can be done by standing the article on the kiln for a time before putting it inside. With a muffle it can be placed on the tray just by the opening and the flame played on it gently from underneath, circling round the edges first and gradually increasing the heat.

When the article is reasonably hot it is put right inside kiln or muffle. With the kiln all that is needed is to inspect through the inspection hole every minute or so until it is seen that the enamel is fused.

With the muffle you continue to play the flame around, never letting it stay too long in one spot lest this becomes overheated. The expanded metal tray will help to spread the flame. When the metal changes colour, increase the heat. You will see the enamel gradually becoming fluid and take on a glassy look. When the metal seems to be glowing through the enamel, fusion is complete.

Have a pair of tweezers or long spatula handy, lift out the piece and check to see that it has been properly fired. If the enamel looks matt, has an orange-peel surface, or contains bubbles, put it back and re-fire; this will not take long since it will still be hot.

Cooling off should always be done as slowly as possible. This is an annealing process which relieves strains, uneven contraction on cooling as between metal and enamel, and so reduces the risk of the enamel cracking.

The article should accordingly be placed on the kiln, or left in the opening of the muffle until it is cool and can be handled for the final inspection.

The final inspection not uncommonly reveals further flaws. In particular, air bubbles may have left pits, or the enamel may have receded from edges, failed to cover some part of the work or spread where it is not wanted. The treatment is re-firing. The edges of the enamel must be roughed which helps to hold the fresh enamel that has to be added, and the piece must then be fired. Pits can be treated by working into the hole with some sharp pointed tool; outer edges should be rubbed with a medium carborundum stone held under running water. Wash well to make sure all loose grains have been removed. If the article is copper or gilding metal, pickle in sulphuric acid and wash. When the article is dry, add fresh enamel where needed and re-fire.

## COUNTER-ENAMELLING

Enamel and metal expand and contract differently under heat. This may result in the enamel cracking, and will almost certainly do so if the metal is flat and less than about $\frac{1}{20}$ inch thick. If the metal is domed and quite thick, then it has so much structural rigidity that there is no risk of any kind of distortion to crack the enamel. With a flat or thin metal the answer is to counter-enamel, that is to say, to enamel the back as well as the top surface.

If one has a kiln, counter-enamelling can be done at the same time as the enamelling. If the work is to be torch-fused, then any counter-enamelling will have to be done as a first process.

If a piece is to be counter-enamelled it should also if possible be domed or have its edges turned down, for then when the time comes to enamel the face, the counter-enamel will be raised and there will be no risk of its sticking to the support. Doming is described on p. 115. To turn down an edge fix a flat-faced punch of suitable shape in the vice and rest the piece on it so that the edge projects about $\frac{1}{8}$ inch and can be hammered down (*135*). The piece should be rotated steadily as the hammering proceeds. Do not attempt to get the edge down completely in one operation but go over it two or three times if necessary.

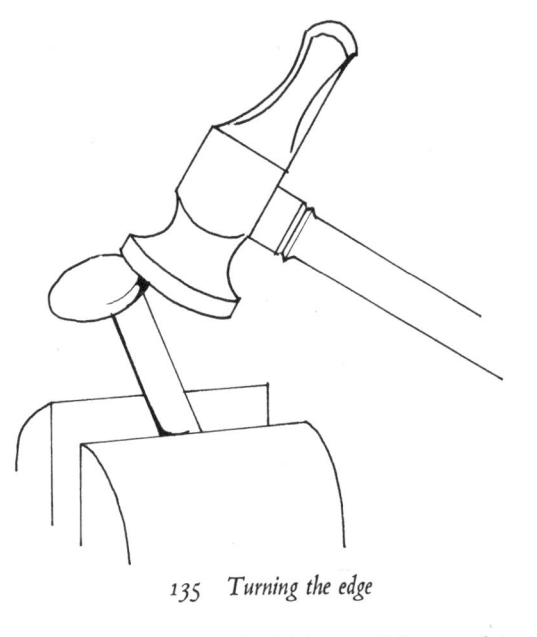

*135   Turning the edge*

The material used can be oddments of powder enamel which can all be stored in one bottle specially for this purpose. Some people save the water in which they have ground and washed their enamels and collect the sludge which settles in due course: this contains impurities, but a good deal of enamel as well, in fact about the weight of enamel ground.

The enamel should be dusted on dry to ensure a very even surface, and ideally should form a layer of the same thickness as that which will be applied subsequently to the front. Firing is done in the same way as already described for ordinary enamelling, but fusion is not carried through to completion: the enamel in fact should only just start to flow and when cooled should present an orange-peel surface. This orange-peel will disappear in subsequent firings.

When the article has been counter-enamelled, it can be turned over and prepared for the proper enamelling. The difficulty now is to devise a support which will ensure that the counter-enamelling does not touch anywhere. If the piece is domed, even though only slightly, it may rest on its edges on the tray with no risk of the counter-enamel coming into contact with and fusing on to any part of the tray. If the doming is not sufficient to be safe, or the piece is flat, some kind of support will have to be made which can grip the sides of the piece. Stout stainless steel wire is ideal for this, being very springy and retaining its toughness sufficiently during the firing. Some supports of this kind are shown (*122–5*), but each support must always be specially formed to suit the shape and size of the work-piece, which it should grip at three points at least. Iron wire will also do, but loses its springiness when heated, and must be painted with rouge as a safeguard against fire scale.

# STONING AND FINISHING OFF

Unless some special effect, involving an irregular surface, is the aim, the enamel should always be level and smooth, for it is then that the colours appear at their most brilliant. This is almost impossible to achieve in the first instance, and indeed with wet-charging quite impossible, for it will only result if the layers of enamel are absolutely level.

The next step after firing is therefore to smooth off the surface by grinding with a carborundum stick. Do this on a wooden board such as a chopping board, and close to a running tap. Begin with a coarse stone, follow up with medium and lastly with a fine grade stone. Stoning is done with a circular motion to avoid causing regular parallel scratches, and with stone and enamel constantly wet. Rinse and dry frequently to see progress. When the whole surface, dry, looks matt and even, with no shiny spot, give a final rinse and a rub with a soft nailbrush to make sure that all loose particles have been removed, then re-fire for the last time.

Incidentally this stoning and re-firing process can also be used to restore transparent enamels which have been burnt and so have lost their colour.

The final step is to buff the enamel on the polishing machine, using a calico mop and a little tripoli, then wash in soap and water.

# A FEW EXAMPLES

## 1 *Black Choker Necklace* (*129*)

There are no cloisons or recesses, and this is therefore a kind of Limoges; but since it lacks the delicate painting of Limoges work, it is perhaps more modestly described as all-over enamel.

The elements are of copper, 10 B.M.G., slightly domed. They measure $1\frac{5}{16}$ inch in length by 1 inch wide at the top (*136*). The necklace is 13 inches long, fitting the average neck, and requires 16 of the shapes to be cut out—this number because they are joined so as to overlap.

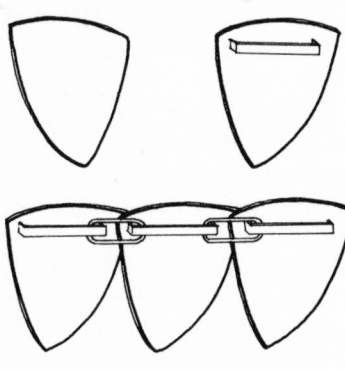

136 *Construction of a necklace:*
*the links*

Dimensions can, of course, be varied, but in any case a circle should be drawn of the right diameter to give whatever length of circumference may be desired, and a few shapes cut out of stiff paper and arranged round the circle. This enables you to determine the number of elements that will be needed, but also the length of the linking bars at the back and the angle at which they must be set. The bars are made of round copper wire, 18 S.W.G., hammered flat and joined by oblong links made of the same wire, not hammered.

Cut out the shapes, true up the edges with a file and dome slightly. Clean the backs with emery paper and mark the points where the bars will be soldered.

Cut the necessary lengths of wire for the bars and bend the ends over at right angles, using flat-nosed pliers. Solder the bars into position, using enamel-ling solder, then boil in sulphuric acid and rinse.

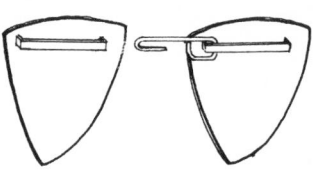

137   *Construction of a necklace: the fastening*

Scrub the back with a wire brush under a running tap, and finish off with the glass brush or burnisher.

Counter-enamel, using a soft-firing opaque colour. For the necklace illustrated a white was used; this was, of course, burned when the front was enamelled in a muffle and turned a dull metallic grey with eccentric but effective patches of white. Do not cover the bars, because any enamel here will only crack off in use. The necklace can be gilded when finished (this will not affect the enamel), or alternatively the bars and the edges of the shapes as well as the links can be polished and covered with clear varnish.

Clean the front of the shapes in the same way as the backs and cover with a soft-firing carbon black enamel which is very rich and dramatic.

Next, the links are made and joined up. They need not be soldered (which would endanger the enamelling) since the wire used is sufficiently stout to hold. The fastening (as indeed the links) remains hidden from view. It consists of a simple ring and hook made of the same wire as the links (137).

## 2  *Cloisonné Cuff-link Ends* (146)

These cuff-link ends measure 1 × ¾ inch and are made of copper sufficiently thick to obviate the need for counter-enamelling, in this case 16 B.M.G.

Draw some flat copper wire to measure 0·6 mm. thick by about 1 mm. wide. This will make the surround and the dividing wires. For the rings a slightly thinner wire, measuring 0·5 × 1 mm. wide, will be needed.

Make up the box-shaped surround to fit exactly along the edges of the piece and solder with enamelling solder. If the piece is to be used for cuff-links, prepare and solder on the link (see p. 99).

Pickle, clean and burnish the front as usual, not neglecting the inside of the surround, then fill in a thin layer of medium flux and fire.

Cut the dividing strips to fit quite tightly into the box and make up (but do not solder) the seven rings. These too should fit quite tightly inside their partitions so that they will support them. Boil the strips and rings in acid and rinse, then using tweezers set all in position in the box, with the strips on edge and kept upright by the rings (138).

Do not add any more enamel but re-fire, and when the flux has become liquid press the partitions and rings into it with the spreader or tweezers. Cool slowly.

Clean again as before, then fill the circles with a thin layer of soft opaque white and the spaces between with soft-firing carbon black enamel, and fire. Repeat until the enamel appears level with the tops of the copper wires. Clean as usual between

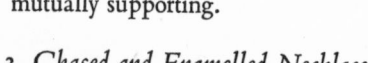

138  *Detail of cuff-link end*

re-firings, but do not pickle because the acid acts on the carbon black enamel.

When the partitions are full, stone until the surface is absolutely level and the enamel matt all over. As it happens, carbon black against copper looks very effective when matt, and the piece can therefore be left thus, with only the copper outer edges and the back to be cleaned on the polishing wheel. But if the polished shiny surface is preferred the piece must of course be re-fired.

It will have been noticed that the partitions and rings are not soldered but are held in position by the enamel, an obvious advantage. This is a common procedure and explains the arrangement of cloisons normally found, that is curves and round shapes, and short straight lengths interrupted by right angles, all set out so as to be self- and mutually supporting.

### 3  Chased and Enamelled Necklace

Champlevé has already been mentioned, a form of enamelling laid in recesses carved out of the metal. In this necklace they have been formed by chasing hollows with a punch on a wooden block.

The links are cut out of silver sheet, 10 B.M.G., and measure $\frac{3}{4}$ inch long by $\frac{1}{4}$ inch wide. The punch, with a rounded face, long and narrow, measuring approximately $\frac{1}{2}$ inch by a little under $\frac{1}{8}$ inch, happened to be available and was just right. But a suitable punch could easily be made at home by filing up the end of a short length of $\frac{1}{4}$ inch square tool steel rod. The place for setting the punch is marked out on the links with a pair of dividers (139).

The block is a short piece of hardwood, actually an offcut 2×2 inches and about 8 inches long, which was fixed in the vice with the end grain at the top. The punch was set on this and struck a fairly heavy blow with the hammer to form a groove corresponding with the punch. The links

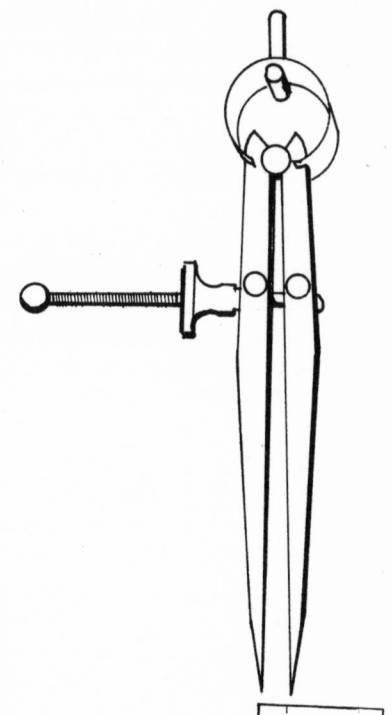

139  *Marking out*

were then laid on the groove, one at a time, the punch set on, carefully lined up and struck with the hammer to form the hollow for enamelling (*140*). This tend-ed to raise the edges of the links, and these were accord-ingly hammered down with the link still in position on the block, so that the hollow should not be damaged. The

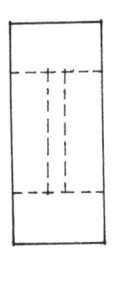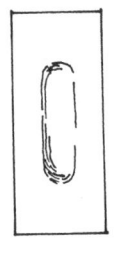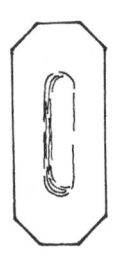

*140   Construction of chased and enamelled
necklace links*

groove in the block gradually became enlarged and worn, and fresh grooves had to be struck from time to time.

When all the links were punched (thirty-four in all), the ends were trimmed and holes for the jump rings marked and drilled, the edges bevelled with a file and the holes smoothed with fine emery paper.

The links were then annealed, pickled, cleaned and enamelled. The colours used for the different links were dark opaque lapis lazuli, soft white, transparent green and two shades of transparent blue.

Using the same or different shaped punches, it is, of course, perfectly possible to punch out and enamel a whole design—which will probably be abstract—on to a larger piece of metal to make, say, a pendant or brooch.

## 4  Champlevé-style Earrings

Another method of achieving a *champlevé* effect is to pierce a pattern in a fairly thin piece of sheet, and to solder this on to a somewhat thicker backing piece (*141*). The pierced holes are thus converted into recesses having sharp edges more nearly like the edges produced by carving or etching, instead of the soft rounded edges left by the punch.

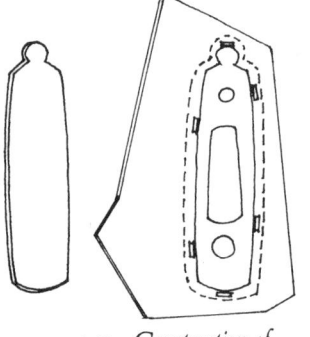

In the example shown the pierced piece was cut from 7 B.M.G. copper sheet and the backing piece from 10 B.M.G.

The two pieces were annealed before being soldered together, and only about 1 mm. from the edges cleaned up all round with emery paper. The object, fairly well achieved, was to discourage the solder from flowing into the recesses, where it would show under the enamel.

The backing piece was cut a little larger all round than the top piece. This excess formed a convenient ledge on which to lay the solder paillons and was filed off when soldering was complete.

*141   Construction of
champlevé-style earring*

All the traditional techniques are still in use today, but in addition much very interesting experimental work is being done which displays an outlook and results quite divorced from the delicate formalisations of the past.

Thus, textured surfaces are produced by piling enamel in small heaps and fusing these, or even by putting an unground lump of frit on to an already enamelled surface, and partially fusing in order to achieve the effect of an uncut stone. Stencils can be used to produce a clearly defined pattern, or alternatively the metal can be wet-charged with several colours flowing freely over the surface to form a loose chance pattern.

Sgraffito is a promising technique sometimes employed. Over a first coat of enamel a second coat of a different colour or colours is dusted or wet-charged and a pattern scratched in this with some kind of pointed tool, such as a nail. The ridges which form on either side of the scratched lines remain after firing. They can then be stoned off or left rough and in either case a thin layer of flux can be fused all over to fill in the scratches. The process can be elaborated still further by laying a series of different colours, scratching, firing and stoning each one so as to produce a design of different coloured lines. With this process it would, of course, be necessary when re-charging to mask off in the earlier layers those lines which are intended to show at the end.

Here are a few experiments:

A copper square, heavy gauge (16 B.M.G.) so as to save counter-enamelling, and cut with a tag at the top which was bent into a ring to make the pendant (147). The square was covered with flux and fused. A smaller copper square of thin sheet (6 B.M.G.) with a round hole cut in the centre was placed on the fluxed surface after painting it thickly with gum tragacanth. This smaller square was also painted with gum and dark blue transparent enamel dusted over the whole and fired. This fixed the smaller square. The photograph shows clearly, though with some exaggeration, the difference in brightness between a transparent enamel fired directly on copper and the same enamel fired on flux.

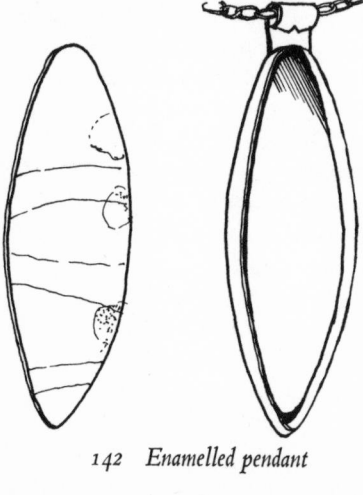

142   *Enamelled pendant*

Next a circle of silver foil was fused into the centre hole, then bright green transparent enamel dusted over this and fired. So that the green enamel should not cover the blue, a simple mask was cut—just a hole of the right size in a piece of paper, and laid over the piece while the green enamel was applied.

Finally, after polishing the whole piece was silver-plated, which gave a nice bright outline to the edges of the two squares and a good finish to the back.

An experiment (142, 148) with transparent and opaque enamels, wet-charged on the metal simultaneously (over previously fired flux) and allowed to flow freely.

Transparent red enamel over flux on copper, counter-enamelled(*150*). The three discs in the centre are gold paillons under a second dusting of red enamel, surrounded by thick edges, to produce a textured effect, of first white opaque then over this an ivy green transparent; wet-charged in order not to have to mask off the red. A little of this white and green enamel on the tip and at the neck of the piece. The links of the chain are enamelled alternately with the red and the ivy green transparent.

## 5 Snowflake Obsidian and Enamel Silver Pendant (67)

This pendant combines a rectangular flat snowflake obsidian, a black stone with white markings, with a rectangular plaque (copper) covered in red transparent enamel with light blobs of opaque orange. The construction is shown in the drawings (*143–4*).

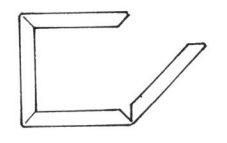

143 *Construction of snowflake obsidian and enamel pendant*

The surround is of flat silver wire, $\frac{1}{8} \times \frac{1}{16}$ inch; inside the right-hand half two blocks of slightly thinner material are soldered to support the plaque so that this lies flush with the surface of the frame.

The plaque reaches exactly from top to bottom of the frame. Its long edges, one of which will remain visible alongside the stone, are turned down at right angles and are also covered with enamel. The plaque is counter-enamelled as a precaution against distortion and to provide a finish at the back. The plaque is glued in position with Araldite.

The ends of the stone are drilled and it is secured by silver nails passing through holes in the frame and soft soldered in position. To make each nail, cut a short length of silver wire of the same size as the hole in the frame and melt one end into a blob as described on p. 95. Insert the wire into a hole of the same size in the drawplate, but from the front, and flatten by gentle hammering. Remove and tidy the shape with a file.

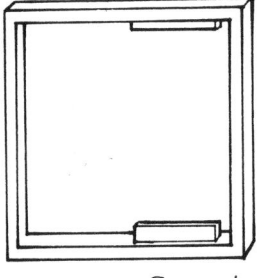

144 *Construction of snowflake obsidian and enamel pendant*

Another example of a pendant combining a stone with enamel is shown(*108*). Here, however, the two plaques of enamel (top) are mounted in bezels like the stone below.

## 6 Enamelled Choker Necklace(*149*)

The links of this copper necklace are covered in a brownish red opaque enamel, with clear red scattered on the surface and opaque white, quite thinly, along the top edge.

The drawing(*145*) shows the shape cut, the outer arms of which were bent round before enamelling to receive the jump rings.

145    *Construction of*
*necklace link*

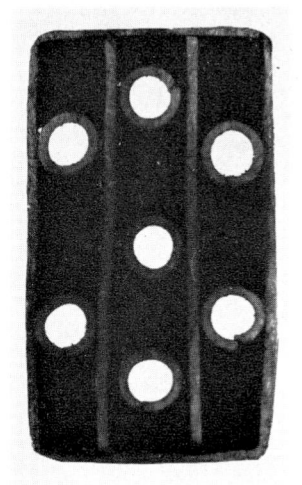

146 Cuff-link end, copper, black and white cloisonné enamel

147 Pendant, copper, silver-plated. Blue and green enamels with silver foil

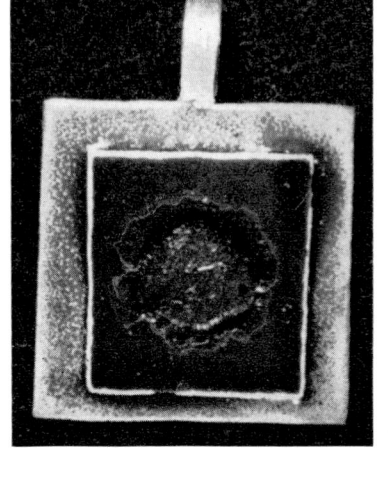

148 Pendant, copper, silver-plated, enamelled

149 Necklace, copper with white and opaque and transparent red enamels

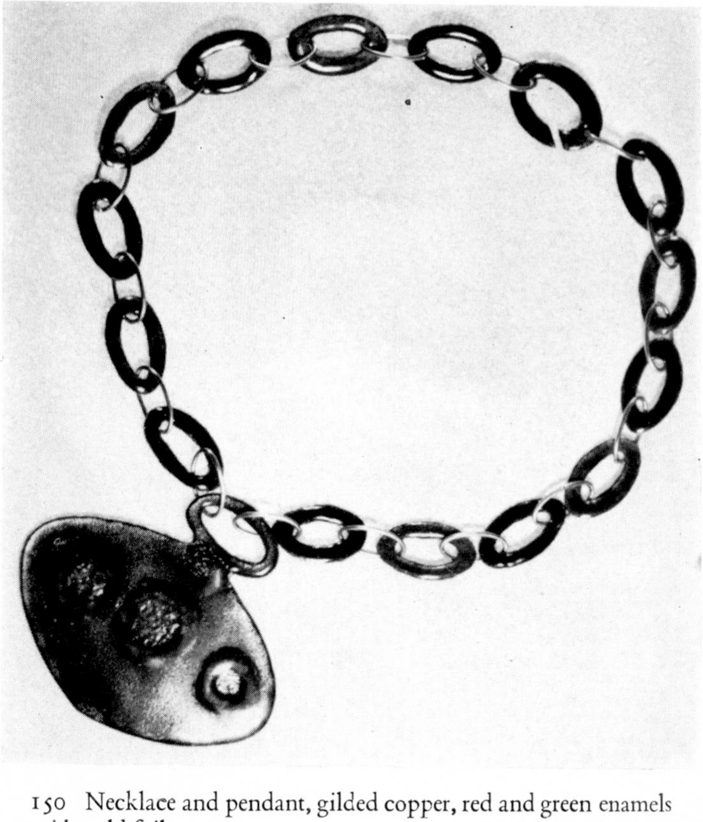

150 Necklace and pendant, gilded copper, red and green enamels with gold foil

# CHAPTER XII
## *Designing Jewelry*

We have described what are the essentially simple techniques of jewelry making. In practising them one learns not only the possibilities, but also the limitations of the tools at our disposal. In handling metals one learns what can and what cannot be done with them, and how their characteristics differ, how for instance a gauge which will be adequate for strength in an article made of copper, may well be excessive if the metal used is silver.

We have also illustrated and described the making of actual articles. They can, but we hope will not, be copied, at least not without modification and development: after all creative work, especially the amateur's who does not have to live by it, should express the ideas and individuality of the person making it. The examples are given so that the beginner may learn how to analyse and solve the problem of construction which each piece of jewelry poses.

All these things are the tools of the trade, necessary experience without which it is not possible to design something that will work, though it may look attractive. A brooch can satisfy every aesthetic instinct, but it will disappoint the wearer if the pin is so set that it does not sit properly. A ravishing ring may be torture if it has sharp edges and projections which cut the adjacent finger.

There remains the question of design, about which so much that is intimidating has been written. Rhythm, harmony, significant form, composition, balance—such expressions abound and are hard to understand. They may become meaningful when related to specific features in a work of art that is before our eyes, but the moment we sit down to produce a design which will express the principles thus learned, the mind becomes a blank, there's not an idea in sight.

The wise man will ignore the golden rules of the classical schools, and he will then be in good company, for this is precisely what the creative artist does. The work comes first, the rules follow, invented by others seeking to explain it, but offering not a bit of help to anyone who wishes to create on his own account.

What, then, will help? Can one sit down and wait for an idea? Well, ideas do not just spring fully armed like Athene from the head of Zeus. A nudge is needed, a starting-point of some kind. This must, of course, be related to whatever may be the essence of what we are trying to create, in this case jewelry. Now a piece of jewelry is an object, and therefore it has shape. That is its essence, unlike a painting whose essence is colour, or a machine whose essence is function.

Every object has shape of some kind, and every object, however far removed it may seem from jewelry, can provide the jeweller with a starting-point. His task is to pick out from a possibly complex shape some element which can be developed for his own purposes. The necklace shown (128) provides a simple illustration. One may like it or not: this is a question of personal taste which matters to no one other than the maker and the wearer. What the necklace illustrates is that it is perfectly simple to take over an ordinary, everyday existing shape and develop this into a piece of jewelry. In this case the links are a copy of an ordinary type of paper-clip, slightly elaborated by lengthening one arm, adding silver beads to the ends and a purely functional rectangular ring at the top, arranged to form a frame for and draw attention to the central stone, and graduated in size to add interest.

All these points are important. The starting-point, the shape, we have already discussed. It is only a starting-point: we develop it (and the development could easily have been carried further), we play around with it, we repeat it in different or the same sizes, we arrange the pieces in some kind of order. The whole thing is really a kind of doodle which—in this case—has been developed into a formal design by repetition. 'In this case' is stressed, since formalisation is by no means necessary. A brooch, for instance, might have been achieved by using a single paper-clip shape, perhaps mounting a stone between the points or within the triangular opening, and the result would have been a free, informal design.

Often our starting-point is something which must actually be built into the piece we are designing, a specially shaped stone for instance which must necessarily condition the design. A very simple example is shown (35), a pendant whose shape was dictated by the shape and markings of the agate which it sets off. But the agate merely determines the general form; within this limitation there is still room for individual ideas in the precise shape of the surround, the method of fixing the stone, and the attachment to the collar.

The shape which is the starting-point is not necessarily an existing shape but one we can make ourselves, merely by playing around with bits of wire and strips of sheet, bending them, twisting them, tying them into knots figuratively speaking. Sooner or later a shape, or an element of a shape will emerge to which something in us responds. It rings a bell, and there is the starting-point. We take that shape, we continue to play with it, modifying it here or there, developing it, perhaps making up similar shapes and arranging them all in a design, or sketching it out on paper and doodling with it, until eventually we arrive at something which is satisfying.

In this field of design the amateur has a great advantage over the commercial jeweller. He does not have to cater for a mass market interested chiefly in the humdrum and the hackneyed, at cut price. He pleases himself, and his friends, and can take time to do so. And if a piece turns out to be a failure he can scrap it, at very little loss to himself. This seems a depressing note upon which to end a book: it is in fact an encouraging one, for it encourages experiment and experiment leads to new discovery.

# APPENDIX I

## *Gauge Comparison Tables*

| Inch | mm. | Birmingham Metal Gauge (Shakespeare's) (B.M.G.) | Standard Wire Gauge (S.W.G.) | Approx. American B. & S. |
|------|-----|-------------------------------------------------|------------------------------|--------------------------|
| ·001 | ·025 | — | 50 | — |
| ·0012 | ·030 | — | 49 | — |
| ·0016 | ·041 | — | 48 | — |
| ·002 | ·051 | — | 47 | — |
| ·0024 | ·061 | — | 46 | — |
| ·0028 | ·071 | — | 45 | — |
| ·0032 | ·081 | — | 44 | 40 |
| ·0036 | ·091 | — | 43 | 39 |
| ·004 | ·102 | — | 42 | 38 |
| ·0044 | ·112 | — | 41 | 37 |
| ·0048 | ·122 | — | 40 | — |
| ·005 | ·127 | — | — | 36 |
| ·0052 | ·132 | — | 39 | 35 |
| ·006 | ·152 | — | 38 | 34 |
| ·0065 | ·165 | — | — | — |
| ·0068 | ·173 | — | 37 | — |
| ·007 | ·178 | — | — | 33 |
| ·0076 | ·193 | — | 36 | — |
| ·008 | ·203 | — | — | 32 |
| ·0084 | ·213 | — | 35 | — |
| ·0085 | ·216 | I | — | — |
| ·009 | ·229 | — | — | 31 |
| ·0092 | ·234 | — | 34 | — |
| ·0095 | ·241 | 2 | — | — |
| ·010 | ·254 | — | 33 | 30 |
| ·0105 | ·267 | 3 | — | — |
| ·0108 | ·274 | — | 32 | — |
| ·011 | ·279 | — | — | 29 |
| ·0116 | ·295 | — | 31 | — |
| ·012 | ·305 | 4 | — | — |
| ·0124 | ·315 | — | 30 | 28 |

| Inch | mm. | Birmingham Metal Gauge (Shakespeare's) (B.M.G.) | Standard Wire Gauge (S.W.G.) | Approx. American B. & S. |
|---|---|---|---|---|
| ·013 | ·330 | — | — | — |
| ·0136 | ·345 | — | 29 | — |
| ·014 | ·356 | 5 | — | 27 |
| ·0148 | ·376 | — | 28 | — |
| ·015 | ·381 | — | — | — |
| ·016 | ·406 | 6 | — | — |
| ·0164 | ·417 | — | 27 | 26 |
| ·017 | ·432 | — | — | — |
| ·018 | ·457 | — | 26 | 25 |
| ·0185 | ·470 | — | — | — |
| ·019 | ·483 | 7 | — | — |
| ·020 | ·508 | — | 25 | 24 |
| ·0215 | ·546 | 8 | — | — |
| ·022 | ·559 | — | 24 | 23 |
| ·024 | ·610 | 9 | 23 | — |
| ·025 | ·635 | — | — | 22 |
| ·027 | ·686 | — | — | — |
| ·028 | ·711 | 10 | 22 | 21 |
| ·030 | ·762 | — | — | — |
| ·032 | ·813 | 11 | 21 | 20 |
| ·033 | ·838 | — | — | — |
| ·035 | ·889 | 12 | — | — |
| ·036 | ·914 | — | 20 | 19 |
| ·038 | ·965 | 13 | — | — |
| ·039 | ·991 | — | — | — |
| ·040 | 1·016 | — | 19 | 18 |
| ·042 | 1·067 | — | — | — |
| ·043 | 1·092 | 14 | — | — |
| ·046 | 1·168 | — | — | 17 |
| ·048 | 1·219 | 15 | 18 | — |
| ·049 | 1·244 | — | — | — |
| ·051 | 1·295 | 16 | — | 16 |
| ·055 | 1·397 | 17 | — | — |
| ·056 | 1·422 | — | 17 | — |
| ·058 | 1·473 | — | — | 15 |
| ·059 | 1·499 | 18 | — | — |
| ·060 | 1·524 | — | — | — |
| ·062 | 1·575 | 19 | — | — |

| Inch | mm. | Birmingham Metal Gauge (Shakespeare's) (B.M.G.) | Standard Wire Gauge (S.W.G.) | Approx. American B. & S. |
|---|---|---|---|---|
| ·064 | 1·626 | — | 16 | 14 |
| ·065 | 1·651 | 20 | — | — |
| ·067 | 1·702 | — | — | — |
| ·069 | 1·753 | 21 | — | — |
| ·072 | 1·829 | — | 15 | 13 |
| ·073 | 1·854 | 22 | — | — |
| ·074 | 1·880 | — | — | — |
| ·077 | 1·956 | 23 | — | — |
| ·080 | 2·032 | — | 14 | 12 |
| ·082 | 2·083 | 24 | — | — |
| ·083 | 2·108 | — | — | — |
| ·086 | 2·184 | — | — | — |
| ·090 | 2·286 | 25 | — | 11 |
| ·091 | 2·311 | — | — | — |
| ·092 | 2·337 | — | 13 | — |
| ·095 | 2·413 | — | — | — |
| ·096 | 2·438 | — | — | — |
| ·100 | 2·540 | 26 | — | — |
| ·102 | 2·591 | — | — | 10 |
| ·104 | 2·642 | — | 12 | — |
| ·109 | 2·768 | — | — | — |
| ·110 | 2·794 | — | — | — |
| ·112 | 2·845 | 27 | — | 9 |
| ·116 | 2·946 | — | 11 | — |
| ·120 | 3·048 | — | — | — |
| ·121 | 3·073 | — | — | — |
| ·124 | 3·150 | 28 | — | — |
| ·128 | 3·251 | — | 10 | 8 |
| ·134 | 3·403 | — | — | — |
| ·136 | 3·454 | 29 | — | — |
| ·144 | 3·658 | — | 9 | 7 |
| ·148 | 3·759 | — | — | — |
| ·150 | 3·810 | 30 | — | — |
| ·160 | 4·064 | — | 8 | 6 |
| ·165 | 4·191 | — | — | — |
| ·166 | 4·216 | 31 | — | — |
| ·167 | 4·242 | — | — | — |
| ·176 | 4·470 | — | 7 | — |

| Inch | mm. | Birmingham Metal Gauge (Shakespeare's) (B.M.G.) | Standard Wire Gauge (S.W.G.) | Approx. American B. & S. |
|---|---|---|---|---|
| ·180 | 4·572 | — | — | 5 |
| ·182 | 4·623 | 32 | — | — |
| ·183 | 4·648 | — | — | — |
| ·192 | 4·877 | — | 6 | — |
| ·200 | 5·080 | 33 | — | — |
| ·201 | 5·105 | — | — | — |
| ·203 | 5·156 | — | — | 4 |
| ·212 | 5·385 | — | 5 | — |
| ·213 | 5·410 | — | — | — |
| ·216 | 5·486 | 34 | — | — |
| ·220 | 5·588 | — | — | — |
| ·232 | 5·893 | — | 4 | 3 |
| ·238 | 6·045 | 35 | — | — |
| ·240 | 6·096 | — | — | — |
| ·249 | 6·325 | — | — | — |
| ·250 | 6·350 | 36 | — | — |
| ·252 | 6·404 | — | 3 | — |
| ·256 | 6·502 | — | — | 2 |
| ·259 | 6·578 | — | — | — |
| ·270 | 6·858 | 37 | — | — |
| ·276 | 7·010 | — | 2 | — |
| ·278 | 7·061 | 38 | — | — |
| ·284 | 7·214 | — | — | — |
| ·289 | 7·341 | 39 | — | I |
| ·300 | 7·620 | 40 | I | — |

# APPENDIX II
## Comparison Table of Ring Sizes

| British | European | American (approx.) | Inside diameter inch | Inside diameter mm. |
|---------|----------|--------------------|------|------|
| A |  |  | ·4750 | 12·055 |
|  | 38 |  | ·4762 | 12·096 |
|  |  | 1 | ·486 | 12·344 |
|  | 39 |  | ·4887 | 12·414 |
| B |  |  | ·4905 | 12·459 |
|  | 40 |  | ·5013 | 12·733 |
| C |  |  | ·5060 | 12·852 |
|  |  | 2 | ·518 | 13·157 |
| D |  |  | ·5215 | 13·246 |
|  | 42 |  | ·5263 | 13·369 |
| E |  |  | ·5370 | 13·640 |
|  | 43 |  | ·5389 | 13·687 |
|  |  | 3 | ·550 | 13·970 |
|  | 44 |  | ·5514 | 14·006 |
| F |  |  | ·5525 | 14·034 |
|  | 45 |  | ·5639 | 14·324 |
| G |  |  | ·5680 | 14·427 |
|  | 46 |  | ·5765 | 14·642 |
|  |  | 4 | ·582 | 14·783 |
| H |  |  | ·5835 | 14·821 |
|  | 47 |  | ·5890 | 14·961 |
| I |  |  | ·5990 | 15·215 |
|  | 48 |  | ·6015 | 15·279 |
|  | 49 | 5 | ·6141 | 15·597 |
| J |  |  | ·6145 | 15·608 |
|  | 50 |  | ·6266 | 15·916 |
| K |  |  | ·6300 | 16·002 |
|  | 51 |  | ·6391 | 16·234 |
| L |  | 6 | ·6455 | 16·396 |
|  | 52 |  | ·6517 | 16·552 |
| M |  |  | ·6610 | 16·789 |
|  | 53 |  | ·6642 | 16·871 |
| N |  |  | ·6765 | 17·183 |

| British | European | American (approx.) | Inside diameter inch | mm. |
|---|---|---|---|---|
|  |  |  | Inside diameter | |
|  |  |  | inch | mm. |
|  | 54 |  | ·5767 | 17·189 |
|  |  | 7 | ·678 | 17·221 |
|  | 55 |  | ·6893 | 17·507 |
| O |  |  | ·6920 | 17·577 |
|  | 56 |  | ·7018 | 17·826 |
| P |  |  | ·7075 | 17·971 |
|  | 57 | 8 | ·7143 | 18·144 |
| Q |  |  | ·7230 | 18·364 |
|  | 58 |  | ·7269 | 18·462 |
| R |  |  | ·7385 | 18·758 |
|  | 59 |  | ·7394 | 18·780 |
|  |  | 9 | ·743 | 18·872 |
|  | 60 |  | ·7519 | 19·098 |
| S |  |  | ·7540 | 19·152 |
|  | 61 |  | ·7644 | 19·416 |
| T |  |  | ·7695 | 19·545 |
|  | 62 |  | ·7770 | 19·736 |
|  |  | 10 | ·778 | 19·761 |
| U |  |  | ·7850 | 19·939 |
|  | 63 |  | ·7895 | 20·054 |
| V |  |  | ·8005 | 20·333 |
|  | 64 |  | ·8020 | 20·372 |
|  |  | 11 | ·811 | 20·599 |
|  | 65 |  | ·8146 | 20·690 |
| W |  |  | ·8160 | 20·726 |
|  | 66 |  | ·8271 | 21·008 |
| X |  |  | ·8315 | 21·120 |
|  | 67 |  | ·8396 | 21·326 |
|  |  | 12 | ·843 | 21·412 |
| Y |  |  | ·8470 | 21·514 |
|  | 68 |  | ·8522 | 21·645 |
| Z |  |  | ·8625 | 21·908 |
|  | 69 |  | ·8647 | 21·963 |
|  |  | 13 | ·875 | 22·225 |

# List of Suppliers

## GREAT BRITAIN

### Smelters and Suppliers of Precious Metals

Johnson Matthey and Co., Ltd.
78 Hatton Garden, London E.C.1.
Vittoria Street, Birmingham.

D. Pennellier & Co., Ltd.
28 Hatton Garden, London E.C.1.

Sheffield Smelting Co., Ltd.
Thessco House, 134–136 St John Street, Clerkenwell, London E.C.1.
Royds Mills, Windsor Street, Sheffield 4.
St Paul's Square, Birmingham.

### Base Metals

J. Smith & Sons (Clerkenwell) Ltd.
42–54 St John's Square, London E.C.1.

### Jewellers' Tools

Charles Cooper, Ltd.
92–93 Hatton Garden, London E.C.1.

E. Gray & Son, Ltd.
12–16 Clerkenwell Road, London E.C.1.
(Also supplies silver in all forms.)

George Panton & Sons
Buchanan Street, Glasgow.

### Precious and Semi-Precious Stones

M. L. Beach
41 Church Street, Twickenham, Middlesex.

C. Calipé
44 Poland Street, Oxford Street, London W.1.

Gemstones
23 Hatton Gardens, London E.C.1.

Gregory Bottley & Co. (Mineralogists)
30 Old Church Street, London S.W.3.

R. E. Couch
30b Great Sutton Street, Clerkenwell, London E.C.1.

A. E. Ward & Son, Ltd. (General Lapidaries)
10 Albemarle Way, Clerkenwell, London E.C.1.

### Enamels

E. Gray & Son, Ltd.
12–16 Clerkenwell Road, London E.C.1.

W. J. Hutton
285 Icknield Street, Hockley, Birmingham.

Thomson & Joseph, Ltd.
46 Watling Street, Radlett, Hertfordshire.

Wengers Ltd.
Etruria, Stoke-on-Trent.

*Gold and Silver Foil*

George M. Whiley, Ltd.
54–60 Whitfield Street, London W.1.

*Kilns*

Catterson-Smith, Ltd.
Adams Bridge Works, South Way, Exhibition Grounds, Wembley.

*Electro Platers & Gilders*

W. Pairpont & Sons, Ltd.
50 Broadwick Street, London W.1.

F. P. Richards
60 Poland Street, London W.1.

*Polishing Equipment and Materials*

Canning & Co.
Great Hampton Street, Birmingham.

## U.S.A.

*Smelters and Suppliers of Precious Metals*

Eastern Smelting & Refining Corp.
107 West Brookline Street, Boston 18, Massachusetts.

Goldsmith Brothers Smelting & Refining Co.
58 East Washington Street, Chicago 2, Illinois.

Handy & Harman
82 Fulton Street, New York 38, N.Y.
330 North Gibson Street, El Monte, California.
141 John Street, Toronto, Canada.

Southwest Refining Co.
P.O. Box 2010, Dallas 21, Texas.

*Base Metals*

T. E. Conklin Brass & Copper Co., Inc.
54 Lafayette Street, New York 13, N.Y.

Patterson Bros.
15 Park Row, New York 7, N.Y.

Vorys Bros., Inc.
834 West Third Avenue, Columbus, Ohio.

*Jewellers' Tools*

Allcraft Tool & Supply Co., Inc.
15 West 45th Street, New York 36, N.Y.

Ernest Linick & Co.
55 Wabash Avenue, Chicago, Illinois.

C. E. Marshall Co.
Box 7737, Chicago, Illinois.

Jewelry Craft Supply
Box 14, Forest Hills 75, N.Y.

Wm. J. Orkin Inc.
373 Washington Street, Boston 8, Massachusetts.

*Gemstones (polished)*

John J. Barny Co.
P.O. Box 15, Detroit 31, Michigan.

International Gem Co.
15 Maiden Lane, New York 7, N.Y.

William Mercer
665 Fifth Avenue, New York 22, N.Y.

Charles Weidinger
631 West 54th Place, Chicago 9, Illinois.

*Roughs*

Grieger's
1633 East Walnut Street, Pasadena 4, California.

V. D. Hill
Route 7, Box 188, Salem, Oregon.

Technicraft Lapidaries Corp.
3560 Broadway, New York 31, N.Y.

Vreeland Manufacturing Co.
4105 North-East 68th Avenue, Portland 13, Oregon.

*Enamels*

B. K. Drakenfeld and Co.
45 Park Place, New York 7, N.Y.

Ferro Enamel Corp.
4150 East 56 Street, Cleveland, Ohio.

Thomas C. Thompson
1539 Deerfield Road, Highland Park, Illinois.

House of Ceramics
2481 Mathews Avenue, Memphis, Tennessee.

Steward Clay Co.
133 Mulberry Street, New York 13, N.Y.

*Metal Foils*

Hastings and Co.
2314 Market Street, Philadelphia 3, Pennsylvania.

C. R. Hill Co.
35 West Grand River, Detroit 26, Michigan.

Goldsmith Bros., Smelting & Refining
111 North Wabash Avenue, Chicago 2, Illinois.

Welsh Gold Stampers
241 Centre Street, New York, N.Y.

*Kilns*

Anchor Tool and Supply Co.
12 John Street, New York, N.Y.

Electric Hotpack Co.
  Coltman Avenue and Melrose Street,
  Philadelphia, Pennsylvania.

Gregory Kilns
  21570 Edgecliff Drive, Cleveland, Ohio.

Skeett and Sons
  2618 South East Steele Street, Portland,
  Oregon.

Pierce Equipment Co., Inc.
  893 Chambers Road, Columbus 12,
  Ohio.

# Bibliography

AULD, J. LESLIE.
*Your Jewellery* Sylvan Press Ltd, London, 1951; Charles A. Bennett Co. Inc., Peoria, Illinois, 1951.

BAERWALD, MARCUS, AND MAHONEY, TOM.
*Story of Jewelry* Abelard-Schuman, New York, 1960.

BATES, KENNETH F.
*Enameling Principles and Practice* The World Publishing Co., Cleveland and New York, 1951; A. Constable and Co. Ltd, London, 1952.

BAXTER, WILLIAM T. L.
*Jewelry, Gem Cutting and Metalcraft* 3rd edition. McGraw-Hill Book Co. Inc., New York, 1950.

BOVIN, MURRAY.
*Jewelry Making* V. C. Bergling, Coral Gables, Florida, 1954.

BRADFORD, E.
*Four Centuries of European Jewellery* Country Life Ltd, London, 1953.
*English Victorian Jewellery* Country Life Ltd, London, 1959.

CELLINI, BENVENUTO.
*The Life of Benvenuto Cellini* Phaidon Press Ltd, London, 1949.

CLEGG, HELEN, AND LAROM, MARY.
*Jewelry Making for Fun and Profit* David McKay Co. Inc., New York, 1951.

CUNYNGHAME, H. H.
*Art Enamelling on Metals* A. Constable and Co. Ltd, London, 2nd edition, 1901.

DALI, SALVADOR.
*A Study of his Art-in-Jewels* The Graphic Society, New York, 1959; Studio Books, London, 1959.

DARLING, A.
*Antique Jewelry* Century House, Watkins Glen, New York, 1953.

DAVIS, MARY L., AND PACK, GRETA.
*Mexican Jewelry* University of Texas Press, Austin, Texas, 1963.

DAY, LEWIS F.
*Enamelling* B. T. Batsford Ltd, London, 1907.

EMERSON, A. R.
*Handmade Jewellery* Dryad Ltd, Leicester, 1955.

153

EVANS, JOAN.
*A History of Jewellery 1100–1870*   Faber and Faber Ltd, London, 1953.

FISHER, ALEXANDER.
*The Art of Enamelling upon Metal*   The Studio, London, 1906.

FRANKE, L. E., AND UDELL, W. L.
*Handwrought Jewelry*   (McKnight) Taplinger, New York, 1962.

HUGHES, GRAHAM.
*Modern Jewelry*   Studio Books, London, 1963.

KRAMER, K., AND N.
*Coppercraft and Silver Made at Home* Chilton Co., Philadelphia, 1957; Pitman Publishing Corp., London, 1958.

KRONQUIST, EMIL F.
*Metalcraft and Jewelry*   Manual Arts Press, Peoria, Illinois, 1926.

LYON, PETER.
*Design in Jewellery*   Peter Owen Ltd, London, 1956.

MARTIN, CHARLES J.
*How to Make Modern Jewelry*   Distributed by Simon and Schuster, Inc., Museum of Modern Art, New York, 1949.

MARYON, HERBERT.
*Metalwork and Enamelling*   Chapman and Hall, Ltd, London, 1912; Dover Publications, New York, 1955.

MILLENET, LOUIS ELIE.
*Enamelling on Metal*   Translated by H. de Koningh, Technical Press Ltd, London, 1947.

MILLER, JOHN G.
*Metal Art Crafts*   2nd edition in preparation. D. Van Nostrand Co. Inc., Princeton, New Jersey, 1962.

MOSELEY, SPENCER; JOHNSON, PAULINA, AND KOENIG, HAZEL.
*Crafts Design*   An illustrated guide. Wadsworth Publishing Co. Inc., Belmont, California, 1962.

NEUMANN, ROBERT VON.
*Design and Creation of Jewelry*   Chilton Co., Philadelphia, 1961; Sir Isaac Pitman and Sons, Ltd, London, 1962.

OTTEN, MITZI, AND BERL, KATHE.
*The Art of Enamelling*   Published by the authors, New York, 1950.

PACK, GRETA.
*Jewelry Making for the Beginning Craftsman* D. Van Nostrand Co. Inc., Princeton, New Jersey, 1957.

RATHBONE, R. LLEWELYN.
*Simple Jewellery*   A. Constable and Co. Ltd, London, 1910.

ROY, V. A.
*Ceramics*   McGraw-Hill Book Co. Inc., New York, 1959.

SANGER, ARTHUR AND LUCILLE.
*Cabochon Jewelry Making*   Charles A. Bennett Co. Inc., Peoria, Illinois, 1951.

SELWYN, A.
*The Retail Jeweller's Handbook*   Heywood and Co. Ltd, London, 1948.

SHOENFELT, J. F.
*Designing and Making Hand Wrought Jewelry*   McGraw-Hill Book Co. Inc., New York, 1960.

SINKANKAS, J.
*Gem Cutting*   D. Van Nostrand Co. Inc., Princeton, New Jersey, 1962.

SMITH, DONALD.
*Metalwork*   B. T. Batsford Ltd, London, 1948.

SMITH, FREDERICK R.
*Small Jewellery*   Pitman Publishing Corp., London and New York, 1951.

SMITH, G. F. HERBERT.
*Gemstones*   Methuen and Co. Ltd, London, 1940.

THOMPSON, THOMAS E.
*Enamelling on Copper and Other Metals*   Thomas C. Thompson Co., Highland Park, Illinois, 1950.

UNTRACHT, OPPI.
*Enamelling on Metal*   Greenberg, New York, 1957; Pitman Publishing Corp., London, 1958.

VICTOR, ARTHUR E., AND LILA M.
*Gem Tumbling and Baroque Jewelry Making*   A guide for amateur tumblers. J. D. Simpson and Co., Spokane, Washington, 1957.

WEINSTEIN, MICHAEL.
*The World of Jewel Stones*   Sheridan House, New York, 1958.

WILSON, H.
*Silverwork and Jewellery*   Sir Isaac Pitman and Sons Ltd, London and New York, 1902.

WINEBRENNER, D. K.
*Jewelry Making as an Art Expression*   International Textbook Co., Scranton, Pennsylvania, 1953.

WINTER, EDWARD.
*Enamel Art on Metals*   Watson-Guptill Publications Inc., New York, 1958.
*Enamelling For Beginners*   Watson-Guptill Publications Inc., New York, 1962.

ZARCHY, HARRY.
*Jewelry-Making and Enamelling*   Alfred A. Knopf Inc., New York.

*Modern British Jewellery*   The Worshipful Company of Goldsmiths, London, 1963.

# INDEX

# Index

The numerals in **Bold** type denote the *Figure* numbers of the illustrations